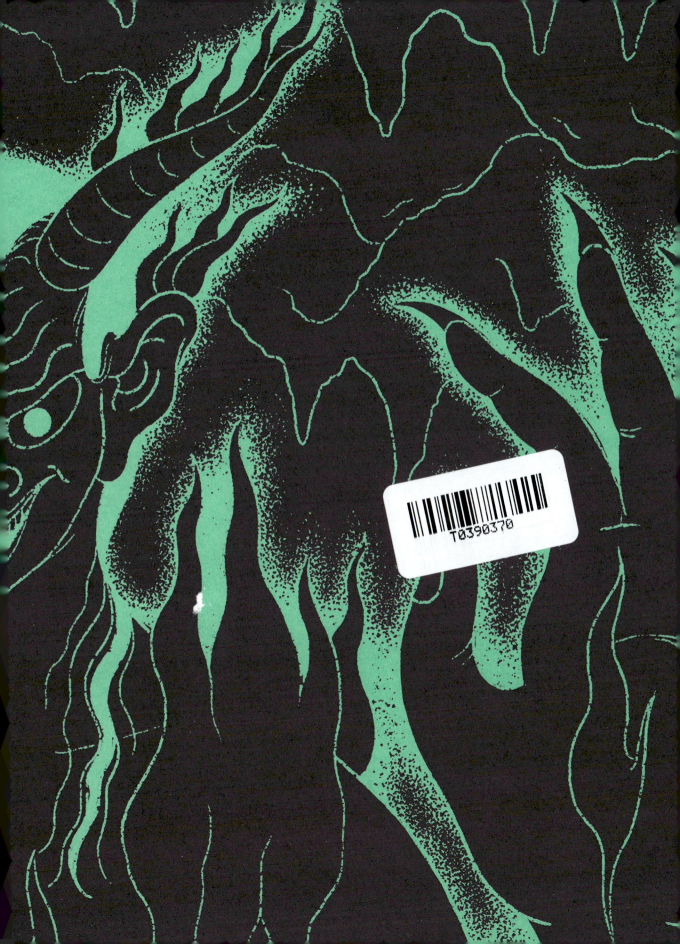

ghostlore

ghostlore

Unveiling 50 phantoms that
have haunted history

WRITTEN BY
ICY SEDGWICK

ILLUSTRATED BY
MABEL ESTEBAN GARCÍA

CONTENTS

Introduction 10

Europe 16

Athenodorus – Greece 18

Draugr – Scandinavia 20

Myling – Scandinavia 24

The Paris Catacombs Ghost – France 26

Barguest – England 28

Dullahan – Ireland 32

Green Lady – Scotland and Wales 36

Strigoi – Romania 40

Santa Compaña – Spain and Portugal 44

Pantafica – Italy 48

Shubin – Ukraine 50

Poltergeist – Germany 52

Asia and Oceania 56

Yūrei – Japan 58

Onryō – Japan 60

Aswang – Philippines 64

Phi Hua Khat – Thailand 68

Jiāngshī – China 70

Yuan Gui – China 74

Naale Baa – India 76

Ifrit – Persia and Egypt 78

Fisher's Ghost – Australia 82

Gwisin – Korea 86

Preta – East Asia 90

The Night Marchers – Hawai'i 94

Sundel Bolong – Indonesia 98

Africa 102

Obambo – Central Africa 104

Adze – Togo, Benin, Ghana, and Nigeria 106

Madam Koi Koi – Nigeria 110

Ogbanje – Nigeria 114

Sasabonsam – Ghana, Togo, and Côte d'Ivoire 116

Popobawa – Zanzibar 118

Uniondale Hitchhiker – South Africa 122

Aïcha Kandisha – Morocco 126

North America and Caribbean 130

Jumbee – Caribbean 132

Duppy – Caribbean 134

Hupia – Caribbean 138

La Ciguapa – Dominican Republic 140

Dungarvon Whooper – Canada 142

Headless Nun – Canada 146

Ridgeway Ghost – USA 150

Greenbrier Ghost – USA 152

Feu Follet – USA 156

Central and South America 158

Homen do Saco – Brazil 160

La Planchada – Mexico 162

La Pascualita – Mexico 166

El Silbón – Colombia and Venezuela 168

La Bolefuego – Colombia and Venezuela 170

Pishtaco – Peru and Bolivia 174

El Peuchen – Chile and Argentina 178

La Mocuana – Nicaragua 182

Resources 186

Glossary 187

Index 188

About the author and illustrator 191

INTRODUCTION

As a researcher of ghosts, and indeed a former ghost hunter, people often ask me when I first saw a ghost. As it happens, I think I've only ever seen one, drifting across a distant room inside Mary King's Close in Edinburgh, but I've always had a staunch conviction that even if I couldn't see them, they were still there. After all, I can't see gravity, but I need only knock something off a table to recognize its effects.

Ghosts have certainly had an effect on literature, art, cinema, theatre, and human experience itself for thousands of years, and I am entirely unsurprised at the ongoing fascination with them here in the Digital Age. Whenever we stumble across the social media page of a dearly departed friend, we may realize that we will each continue to haunt the internet after we leave the mortal plane—albeit as pixels rather than ectoplasm.

So this, my friends, is a book of ghosts, spirits, and monsters. You may wonder, what exactly is the difference between spirits, ghosts, fairies, and monsters? In some ways, it is merely a matter of terminology. For the last couple of centuries, people in the West have had a fascination with categorizing and labeling phenomena to better understand it. The problem with this is that many spirits blur the boundaries we're so intent on erecting. Poltergeists and brownies share a lot of common behavior, and scholars still debate the link between fairies and the dead in folklore from the Celtic nations. To make matters easier, we'll consider these stories through the lens of the supernatural, defined by Merriam-Webster as being both "of or relating to an order of existence beyond the visible observable universe" and "departing from what is usual or normal especially so as to appear to transcend the laws of nature". Basically... things get weird.

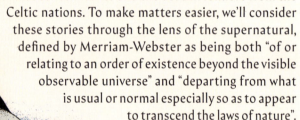

Introduction   Icy Sedgwick

Some of the ghosts in this volume are the spirits of the dead, kept earthbound through a desire for justice, revenge, or even to help people, like La Planchada (p.162). Other ghosts are like the onryō (p.60), twisted through the circumstances of their death into a terrifying spirit, or

10

made monstrous through whatever happened to them in life. Yet others are more ancient spirits, haunting locations that are important to them, like forests or mountains, feared by humans for their fondness for mischief or mayhem. Some of these spirits may do you the favor of warning you of their approach, often with whistling or chittering sounds that stir the primal part of your brain into action—though this will be the only kindness such fierce spirits will grant you.

While some represent a specific type of spirit, such as the preta (p.90), others are examples of a ghost story found all over the world, like the phantom hitchhiker or the wronged woman who appears to a family member in a dream after their death to make sure the truth of their demise is known. These story categories are globally common, often colored by the context of their location or the time in which they're said to have happened, and the commonality of such stories suggests a deep fascination with them by the living. Some stories have passed along trade routes or crossed borders between neighboring countries, which may explain the common trope of the long-haired female ghost in East Asia. And some stories may have influenced those that came after them, with the stories haunting each other, the ghost of one tale inspiring the ghost of another.

Introduction Icy Sedgwick

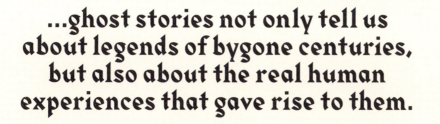

...ghost stories not only tell us about legends of bygone centuries, but also about the real human experiences that gave rise to them.

It can be tempting to see the appearance of similar ghosts worldwide as a suggestion of a common human existence. On one hand, this is true: humans everywhere feel joy, fear, disappointment, and pain. On the other hand, stories bear the fingerprints of the cultures that created them and may reveal perspectives on history that would otherwise be lost. In these cases, such ghost stories not only tell us about legends of bygone centuries, but also about the real human experiences that gave rise to them. Look at Aïcha Kandisha (p.123), feared now as a terrifying spirit seductress of men, but once a brave freedom fighter determined to resist a colonial force.

Many of these stories act as a cautionary tale, counseling those who hear them to avoid lonely places, to treat people kindly, or to show respect for the dead. Where people follow such advice, they may indeed walk safely through dangerous territory. But if they deviate... Well, the spirits can and will make an example of the unwary and foolhardy.

Of course, in many places, such stories are no mere cautionary tales, designed to encourage safe or proper behavior. The stories encode information about how to survive the onslaught of a colonizing newcomer, which is far more easily transmitted through the medium of storytelling. Yet when viewed from an animist perspective (one which sees a spirit in all things, a perspective that was common throughout human history and is still practiced within Indigenous societies), these spirits and monsters are very real inhabitants of their chosen locations—albeit inhabitants to whom you may wish to give a wide berth.

Still, while these stories tell us a lot about their home culture, they also tell us much about what it means to be human. After all, ghosts are a reminder that we too shall die, known as a *memento mori*, and death is the most fundamental (and guaranteed) thing that we have in common as humans. How shall we face that death? Bravely? Tentatively? Running screaming in the opposite direction?

So, come and sit with me by the campfire in our shared imagination, as we retell these stories of vengeful ghosts, benevolent spirit helpers, and fearsome monsters lurking in the shadows. Just be careful not to peer too hard into the darkness beyond our camp, lest something decides to peer back at you...

Introduction 💀 Icy Sedgwick

Introduction 💀 Icy Sedgwick

CHAPTER 1

Europe

ATHENODORUS

You doze in your chair, a warm breeze drifting in through the open window. You can't believe your luck; the rent for this place is so low! But what was that? You ease yourself out of both sleep and the chair, listening hard. There it is again: a clanking of metal on metal. Before you can leave the room, a pale figure appears in the doorway. He wears tattered clothes and shackles around his wrists and ankles. Is he... beckoning to you?

It seemed only right to start this volume with one of the earliest recorded ghost stories, dating from ancient Greece. Pliny the Younger originally told the story about an encounter between the Greek Stoic philosopher Athenodorus Cananites and a ghost. Athenodorus rented a house in Athens and within days of moving in, strange sounds of groaning and rattling echoed through its corridors at night. The sounds kept Athenodorus awake, yet when he investigated, he found nothing. He reasoned that if he saw nothing when the noises woke him up, then he might have better luck if he was already awake. He stayed up later than usual, working on his book of philosophy.

At the time the noises usually woke him, he again heard rattling chains, this time coming in his direction. He peered into the shadows and made out a spectral figure moving towards him. It gestured for Athenodorus to follow, although Athenodorus gestured for the figure to wait. The figure hung around in his study while Athenodorus finished his writing for the evening. After putting away his work, he held his lantern high and followed the figure out of the study. It led him through the darkened corridors of the house and out into the courtyard, drifted to a particular spot, and then vanished in front of him. Athenodorus marked the spot where the ghost disappeared and retired to bed. For the first time since he'd moved in, he slept soundly, undisturbed by unearthly groans and rattling chains.

The next morning, he went to see the local authorities to request permission to dig in the courtyard. They granted permission and returned to the house with him to help. You won't be surprised to learn they found human remains, with shackles tangled up with the skeleton, still fastened around the wrists. The authorities removed the shackles and the remains, and held a proper burial for the skeleton. Following the funeral, Athenodorus never experienced another disturbance in the house.

We'll never know if the story was true. Irish Stoic Enda Harte suggests Athenodorus intended the story as a parable, demonstrating the power of rational thinking and calm actions over the unknown. Yet the story trope passed into legend, found in ghost stories throughout history before it made its way into novels, plays, and movies. It seems ironic that a potential teaching moment about the power of rational thinking has instead formed the template for countless tales of the supernatural.

DRAUGR

You approach the barrow with curiosity, smartphone in hand, camera app at the ready. The barrow reeks of history, having lain here for centuries—the final resting place of a noble chieftain. The guidebook says it was never looted, which explains why visitors aren't allowed inside. Still, getting up close has made it worth the trip already. Except… the barrow doesn't just reek of history—what is that awful stench? You get closer, aware the temperature has dropped several degrees even though you're not in the shade. Something growls. You look round, but see no other visitors, let alone one with a dog. A door opens in the barrow where there had previously been no door, and a long hand—more claw than finger, with pale blue skin and seeping sores—pokes out into the sunshine. You flee, not wanting to see the creature such a hand belongs to.

This would be a draugr, one of the feared undead creatures in Scandinavian folklore, where they're also called dréag or draugen. The draugr aren't ghosts; they're reanimated corpses, often referred to as revenants, who eat the living—similar to zombies, although the draugr are possessed by ferocious spirits intent on carnage.

They're often described as being blue, black, or deathly pale, carrying the stench of decomposition with them. If their eyes remain, they're luminescent and burn like blue embers. Not only do they have supernatural strength, but they can also change size and shape at will. In Icelandic lore, the draugr could take the form of a cat that sat on a person's chest while they were asleep. The cat got heavier throughout the night until the victim was asphyxiated, something which could be scientifically explained by sleep paralysis.

Draugr started life as high-status living humans, interred in burial mounds with their treasure. Guarding these treasures after death seems to be their main purpose—and given the number of incidents of people breaking into graves, you can see why the draugr would be concerned about their belongings. According to archaeologist Molly Wadstål, most grave mounds show evidence of having been opened.

Draugr · Scandinavia

The draugr aren't ghosts; they're reanimated corpses… possessed by ferocious spirits intent on carnage.

The 14th-century Grettir's Saga tells the tale of an 11th-century Icelandic outlaw, Grettir Ásmundarson, who broke into several burial mounds to steal treasure. Given his success elsewhere, the idea of breaking into another mound in Norway scared him little. Yet Kárr inn gamli, the chieftain buried in the mound, had become a draugr. Grettir battled Kárr and won, even walking away with some of Kárr's grave goods. Grettir's bounty might sound aspirational, but archaeologist Molly Wadstål suggests that the draugr could be a cautionary tale to warn people away from looting burial mounds. That at least explains the draugr that guard their tombs. Leave them alone, and they'll leave you alone.

Yet other draugr seem driven to create chaos for the sake of chaos. Dying a dishonourable death, being a criminal, not being buried properly, dying on the battlefield but not being chosen for Valhalla, or being cursed during life could also see you transform into the draugr after death. These draugr seem unconnected with their burial mounds, preferring instead to spread their evil wherever they can. These are also cautionary tales, encouraging people to avoid dishonest behaviors in life. Such was the fear of draugr that bodies may be pinned in the grave, or the feet tied together to keep them from moving around. Large boulders might be laid on the grave to prevent the draugr crawling free to wreak havoc.

The fate of the draugr befalls another character in Grettir's Saga, Glámr the woodcutter. After refusing to fast on Christmas Day and demanding meat from his wife, he goes to watch a flock of sheep for a neighbor. When he does not return the next day, locals go in search of him. They eventually find his horribly mangled body further up the mountain. Except Glámr doesn't remain dead. He returns the next night and kills those around him, both human and animal alike. Since any person killed by a draugr becomes a draugr themselves, this could explain Glámr's grisly fate—although the saga is at pains to point out his socially unacceptable behaviour before his death. Grettir later kills Glámr, although he ends up cursed with bad luck, loneliness, and nyctophobia, as predicted by Glámr during their fight.

Players of *The Elder Scrolls V: Skyrim* will be

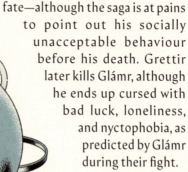

Draugr 💀 Scandinavia

22

familiar with the draugr. J. R. R. Tolkien also drew on the draugr myths for the barrow wights in his *Lord of the Rings* novels. They don't appear in the films by Peter Jackson, but the episode featuring them in the novels is especially harrowing: the hobbits end up trapped in the Barrow-downs with a barrow-wight. After being rescued by Tom Bombadil, the hobbits arm themselves with weapons they find in the barrows, referencing the old legends of draugr guarding their grave goods.

In Icelandic lore, the draugr could take the form of a cat that sat on a person's chest while they were asleep.

MYLING

You walk along the path through the trees, marvelling at how these gentle giants soar far above the forest floor. Suddenly, you hear a strange sound, like a newborn muttering before it breaks into a heart-rending cry. The wail, one with anguish buried deep at its core, echoes around you, weaving through the trees...

The myling is the ghost of a murdered newborn in Scandinavian folklore. These unfortunate babies died at the hands of their unmarried mothers, victims of a society that stigmatized and withdrew support from women pregnant outside of marriage. The mothers often buried their unnamed babies in secret, and never in consecrated ground. As the children weren't baptized or buried with Christian funeral rites, their souls ended up in limbo, caught between our world and the next. In some legends, the ghosts punished their mothers by driving them mad with guilt, or they drew attention to their mother's crime, revealing the illicit pregnancy and infanticide to the community.

Even after punishing their mother, the myling continued to haunt the living, since the lack of the correct funeral rites kept the ghost earthbound. Some ghosts lurked near their burial place, screaming at passersby. Other mylings lay in wait to lead people astray in the dark. An Icelandic belief claimed a person would go mad if a myling crawled three circles around them on one elbow and one knee. Yet people could help the ghost pass over by baptizing the myling. In one Norwegian tale collected in the early 1930s, a myling haunted a remote valley, crying in the undergrowth. It tormented a local man, Petter Nilso, alternating between crying whenever he passed and begging him to free it from its torment, pleading to be baptized and laid to rest in consecrated ground. One autumn evening, Petter headed home along the valley, where the lamenting voice moaned and mewed at him. Eventually, the voice grew so loud it dislodged rocks from the cliffs, and one rock rolled at Petter. The rock shrank to the size of a baby's head, and when it stopped at his feet, it morphed into a baby that crawled up his leg, begging Petter to save it. Finally, Petter carried the baby down to a stream, where he baptized the child Jord-Mattis. When he made the sign of the cross over the child, the ghost vanished and was never heard again.

It's likely that these stories were invented as a cautionary tale to warn women of the consequences of pregnancy outside of marriage or withholding a Christian burial. The father faces no punishment for his part in the pregnancy, with the mother bearing the entire brunt of the social stigma. The myling remains a fragment of these bygone times—but a fragment that still resonates with women around the world who face social challenges for having children outside of marriage.

Myling — Scandinavia

THE PARIS CATACOMBS GHOST

You make your way along the limestone passageway towards a small chamber. The words "Arrête! C'est ici l'empire de la mort!" (Halt! Here is the empire of the dead) appear in black letters on the stone lintel over the doorway. Beyond, you can see stacks of bones, topped by grinning skulls that gleam in the electric light. You hesitate, until you feel a gentle hand on your shoulder, guiding you through the doorway. You turn, expecting to see a kindly tourist helping you over your nerves, but there is no one there. No one who you can see, at least.

In 1763, a public health crisis erupted in Paris, caused by the overflowing burial grounds around the city. King Louis XV banned urban burials in an effort to alleviate the problem, but the church opposed the move. In 1780, heavy rains caused the wall of Cimetière du Les Innocents to collapse, dumping corpses into a neighboring yard. The authorities finally admitted they had a problem. Someone remembered the miles of old lime quarries lying far beneath the city and suggested them as a good alternative to churchyard burials. A section was consecrated by 1786, and by 1788, they'd finished moving the bodies from Les Innocents to the quarries. The authorities moved the bones from other cemeteries to the catacombs.

For a space so associated with death, it only seems natural that the tunnels are said to be haunted. During the French Revolution, Philibert Apsairt worked as a porter at the Val-de-Grâce hospital. He wanted to reach the Chartreux hospital's cellar to access their famous liqueur and decided to use the catacombs as a shortcut. Philibert made his way down a staircase in the hospital courtyard into the tunnels and was never seen again. Not alive, at least. Philibert ended up wandering in the tunnels, disorientated by the similarity of the passageways. He couldn't find the way out, and when his candle sputtered and died, Philibert was doomed in the darkness. Someone stumbled across his body 11 years later in 1804, identifying him from his hospital key ring.

According to legend, his body lay just feet away from an exit. Whoever found him buried him in the catacombs where he was discovered, and some think his ghost still wanders the tunnels. Philibert is said to protect anyone wandering in the catacombs, although no one is sure what he is protecting them from. While there have been more recent stories of people getting lost in the catacombs, thankfully they always make their way to safety, so perhaps Philibert is still doing his staunch duty in the darkness beneath the City of Light.

BARGUEST

You walk along a narrow country lane, dusk shadows pooling beneath the trees. Your rental cottage isn't far and you'll be back before dark. A moment later, a strange sound echoes along the road, turning your blood to ice in your veins. Was that... a howl? You turn and look behind you, and what you see prompts you to shove your way into the nearest hedge. A huge black dog, not quite a mastiff but not a German shepherd, marches along the tarmac, its eyes burning like coals in the twilight. A parade of other dogs scurry, stride, and bound behind it. They ignore you as they pass, but the sight of a spectral funeral bier behind them sends you running for your cottage as soon as they disappear around the bend.

Often thought to take the form of a spectral black dog, the barguest most often appears in the folklore of northern England. It makes appearances in the legends of Northumberland, Durham, and Yorkshire, and occasionally Lancashire and Cumbria.

Most often, the barguest appears in tales as a death omen. One legend saw a barguest haunt the countryside near Leeds, taking the form of a huge black dog with flaming eyes before anyone important died in the area. Having assumed its canine form, it led a procession of local dogs through the neighborhood. If anyone got in their way, the barguest would strike them down, inflicting a wound that never healed. In the 19th century, one man from Yorkshire saw the procession as a child before the death of the local squire.

> **Often thought to take the form of a spectral black dog, the barguest most often appears in the folklore of northern England.**

Yet the nature of the barguest is often the source of some contention. Barguests are also shapeshifters, and descriptions of them differ depending on who you ask. Noted fairy folklorist Katharine Briggs describes it as a bogey-beast, with claws, horns, and fiery eyes, while others name it as a sprite, spectral hound, or a goblin dog. They're most often associated with small villages, lonely roads, or hills. It's rare to hear of them in cities—though given the barguest's love of defying convention, it's probably only a matter of time before that happens.

One barguest near Darlington could take the form of a white cat, a black dog, a headless woman, and a headless man who disappeared in a flash of flame. In Kendal, the barguest took the form of a pig that rattled chains, a pig with eyes like saucers, and a headless woman in white who wandered around the marketplace carrying a tankard. These different forms underline how tricky the barguest is to define. In some places, no one ever saw the barguest; they only heard its horrendous howling or dreadful screams.

> **In some places, no one ever saw the barguest; they only heard its horrendous howling or dreadful screams.**

While some even consider the barguest a demonic spirit, it's also fond of practical jokes and making mischief, which makes it closer to fairy folk. A 19th-century story saw a barguest prowling around Church Street in Whitby in the form of a white pig. A little like the banshee, seeing this barguest foretold a death in your family. Yet it also had a mischievous side, irritating pedestrians on the thoroughfare. If someone walked along Church Street on the pavement, it would force them towards the wall. If the person walked in the road to avoid the barguest, it followed them until they reached the loneliest stretch of the road, where it vanished.

Some writers keep the barguest separate from a similar creature known as the Padfoot. This entity was most common near Leeds, usually described as a black creature about the size of a small donkey with shaggy hair and eyes the size of saucers. The Padfoot followed people at night, gaining its name by padding alongside or behind travelers. Many tales see the Padfoot as a death omen, and it was important to leave it alone if you encountered one because it gained power over you if you spoke to it or struck it. One man kicked the Padfoot, and it dragged him through a hedge and a ditch, before dumping him under his window. Other writers think the Padfoot and the barguest are the same creature.

The differences in its descriptions and names are inevitable since the boundary between the categories of "fairy" and "ghost" is so fluid. The barguest isn't a spectral hound (a phrase normally used in tales of ghost dogs seeking their masters). Yet they also don't fit what we think of when we say "fairy". That in itself is a loaded term, with the image of fairies so much more sanitized and infantilized over the centuries. The barguest's fondness of pranks and mischief, suddenly vanishing without warning, certainly fits with tales of other mischief-loving fairies. But let's not forget that it also acts as a death omen for the families of those who saw it, and is able to inflict supernatural wounds that cannot be healed with mortal medicine, so it's not exactly a fun being.

One thing is certain. If you ever encounter a barguest, leave it to its business, and hopefully, it won't follow you home.

Barguest

England

31

DULLAHAN

The Halloween party draws to a close, with fond goodbyes doled out like the trick-or-treat sweets still left over. You head out into the darkness, ready for the short walk back to your flat. According to your watch, it is now almost midnight, and you're looking forward to the safety of All Saints' Day, just a few moments away. As you hurry along the street, a deep rumbling sounds behind you. You daren't look; you've heard the stories, and you know that nothing good will come of a stolen glance. Before you can turn, a horse thunders past you, its hooves striking up flames against the tarmac. Its rider unleashes a howl not meant for human ears, and the shock hits you that the figure holds aloft his own head...

The figure of the headless horseman is a familiar one, thanks to his appearance in adaptations of Washington Irving's 1820 short story, "The Legend of Sleepy Hollow". Yet this headless horseman predates Irving's story, appearing in Irish folk tales as the Dullahan, roaming the land looking for victims.

Stories differ as to how he lost his head; some think he was a soldier decapitated during battle, now searching for what he lost. Other stories say he still possesses his head, but seeks others to join him in death. In these versions, he holds his head aloft as he rides, looking for victims with his glowing eyes. He holds a spine as a whip in his other hand, which he uses to blind people as he passes. Descriptions of the Dullahan's head always stress the vicious grin stretched across his face, and the skin as being akin to moldy cheese in terms of both texture and color.

Most stories describe him as either riding a similarly headless black horse or riding in a coach made of coffins pulled by a team of six black horses. The horses breathe fire from their noses and strike up fire on the ground as they run. It certainly makes for a lasting impression.

> ### He holds his head aloft as he rides, looking for victims with his glowing eyes.

The Dullahan races across the country, with locked gates opening to let him pass. Each time he rides, he can only speak the name of his victim, and he can only say it

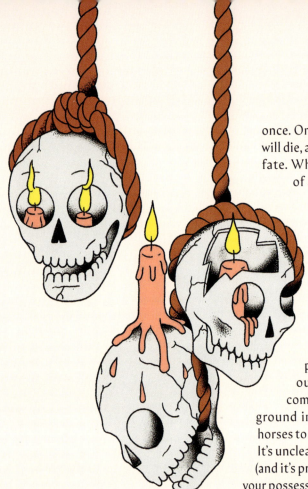

once. Once he says their name, that person will die, and they won't be able to avoid their fate. While figures like the banshee warn of an impending death in the family they're linked to, the Dullahan causes the death without warning. There is also little rhyme or reason as to why he takes those he does.

The Dullahan is active after sunset on particular feast days, causing people to avoid looking outside for fear of seeing him as he passes. If you did find yourself outside after dark and heard him coming, you could throw gold onto the ground in his path, which would force his horses to stop and run in the other direction. It's unclear why gold prompts such a reaction (and it's probably not something you'd have in your possession), but it provides a unique way to ward off the terrifying figure.

Thomas Crofton Croker included the Dullahan in his 1825 book, *Fairy Legends and Traditions of the South of Ireland*, and he emphasized the importance of the death coach to the overall phenomenon. In one poem, he describes the wheel spokes being made from the femurs of dead men, while skulls hang from the coach as lamps. The rumbling made by the coach as it draws near is somehow just as frightening as the awful vision of the headless horses and human remains used to make the carriage.

There is also little rhyme or reason as to why he takes those he does.

In *Fairy and Folk Tales of the Irish Peasantry*, published in 1888, W. B. Yeats suggested that the Dullahan's horrifying coach sometimes accompanied the banshee. That said, we should be careful about relying on Yeats as a source. As fairy expert

Morgan Daimler explains, Yeats collected folklore in the late 19th century, but he reshaped it before sharing it, influencing the tales with his own ideas.

Some believe the Dullahan embodies the Irish god Crom Dubh. Morgan Daimler explains that his name might mean "black stooped one" or "dark croucher", and he may be another variation of the god Crom Cruach. Before Christianization, Crom would battle the god Lugh for access to the bounty of the harvest. Some sources suggest that people offered Crom a sacrifice of their own children to ensure a good harvest. After Christianization, such sacrifices stopped, and the Dullahan appears, perhaps still seeking his annual sacrifice with his nocturnal visits. Given Crom's association with Samhain, it's likely this would be a good evening to stay indoors and avoid the Dullahan.

Dullahan 💀 Ireland

GREEN LADY

You stand in the drafty chamber of the ancient castle, the tapestries on the wall doing little to keep out the chill. A costumed guide points out the finer features of the room and discusses how courtiers would have once waited hours for admittance to this room to meet the queen. You stopped listening several minutes ago, your attention stolen by the striking young woman in the green dress drifting around the room. She ignores everyone, wringing her hands and muttering to herself. It's only as she glides past you that you realize you can see the rest of the room through her…

The green lady is a spirit who defies easy classification, although she only occurs in the British Isles, most notably in Scotland and Wales. She has some crossover with the glaistig of Scottish legend, a female spirit usually found in the Highlands who protected the home and whichever family who lived there. If the family moved out, the glaistig protected the next family to move in. Farmers believed these spirits also protected cattle by leading them to safety before a storm broke, or stopping them from being stolen. A glaistig might turn up at a house, soaked to the skin, asking for shelter. If the family let her in so she could warm up, she stayed to watch over their home.

In other stories, the glaistig was once a mortal noblewoman who wished to become a fairy. The fairies granted her wish, and she became the glaistig. In other legends, a fairy curses the mortal noblewoman with immortality but the legs of a goat that she hides beneath her flowing green dress. Green often appears in folklore as a color favored by the fairies.

Green ladies also have a range of origin stories, but are certainly not as unproblematically benevolent as their glastig cousins. There is a green lady who protects Skipness Castle, which stands by Loch Fyne on the Kintyre peninsula, on the west coast of Scotland. Construction began in the early 13th century and continued until the 16th century. Legends describe the green lady as being child-sized with blonde hair. A helpful spirit, she cleaned and tidied around the castle, even feeding the hens, although allegedly her slightly obsessive nature led her to almost kill a man for sleeping in the wrong bed.

In one tale, a rival clan planned to attack the castle but the green lady used her supernatural powers to confuse them. They scattered and left the area, their wits only returning when they got beyond her reach. The clan tried to head back to the castle, but the confusion also returned. The castle has been empty since the 17th century, but perhaps the green lady remains to protect the property.

Green Lady Scotland and Wales

37

Other stories describe green ladies more simply as the ghosts of women who died while wearing a green dress. This spectral form of green lady can act as a portent of doom, either for the family with which they're associated, or for whoever sees her.

> **Some consider her a bad omen because sightings have been followed by awful happenings—such as fires breaking out—though there have also been sightings by soldiers stationed at the castle that weren't followed by disaster.**

One of the most famous spectral green ladies haunts Scotland's Stirling Castle. According to the legend, she was a servant to Mary Queen of Scots. She had a premonition of disaster befalling the queen, and Mary allowed the servant to spend the night in her bed-chamber to watch over her. The maid lit a taper to keep the shadows at bay but she fell asleep. She was only woken by the smell of smoke and the brightness of the flames. The servant struggled to wake the queen, and though she eventually got Mary to safety, she couldn't survive the flames licking her green dress.

The fire appears in the castle records, though there's no written evidence of the maid. She's been seen around the castle, and some speculate she's looking for her mistress. Some consider her a bad omen because sightings have been followed by awful happenings—such as fires breaking out—though there have also been sightings by soldiers stationed at the castle that weren't followed by disaster.

The 16th-century Crathes Castle in Aberdeenshire also boasts a spectral green lady. She paces back and forth near the fireplace in a room now known as the

Green Lady

Scotland and Wales

38

Green Lady's Room. Sometimes she appears alone; other times she holds an infant. Even Queen Victoria reported seeing a green mist float across the space. The mist picked up a child-sized spectral figure before the pair disappeared into the fireplace.

No one knows her identity, but one version suggests she was a 17th-century servant who became pregnant by one of the Burnett family who owned the castle. In another version, the girl was one of the laird's (owner's) daughters who became pregnant by a stableboy. She disappeared soon after her father discovered her condition.

Either way, in the 1800s, workmen discovered the skeletons of a woman and child beneath the hearthstones during renovations, leading many to question the woman's fate. Visitors note a sense of dread or extreme cold when they enter her room, and if she's seen, it can herald danger, or even death, for the Burnett family, whose line continues today. You can imagine the worry in 2016 when visitors to the castle thought they captured her in the background of a family photo.

When we look at the green lady as a ghost, her story contains so much violence or sadness, which may explain why seeing her sometimes heralds more doom. Yet when we look at her as a fairy, she's a benevolent force, protecting the home from outside threats. It proves how difficult some of these categories can be, though thankfully, there's enough room in the space between ghost and fairy for both types of green lady to exist.

Green Lady 💀 Scotland and Wales

STRIGOI

A news story blares on TV while you make breakfast. It seems a group of men in the next village have had to take action against a strigoi—popularly, but not accurately, called a vampire. You watch the footage in amazement, a crowd of police officers guarding the open grave. Photos flick on screen, showing a "before" shot of a beautiful young woman, and the "after" shot of her frail, gaunt form. The locals blame her late grandmother, and you cannot imagine the sweet old woman shown in the report as being any kind of monster. But appearances can be deceptive.

According to vampire writer Camela Thompson, there are two forms of strigoi: the strigoi viu, or living strigoi; and the strigoi mort, or undead strigoi. The former are born with certain qualities that are supposedly cursed, such as having red hair, being born in the caul (amniotic sac), having a birth defect, or being the seventh child of the same sex as the preceding six. While living strigoi don't always have supernatural abilities, there is a fear they may return from the grave as undead strigoi.

Banish the idea of a body hauling itself out of a grave. The strigoi mort first returns as a form of poltergeist, wreaking havoc in their family home. (This is the reason why many European burial customs see people "confuse" the spirit so it can't return to its home after the funeral, by taking a meandering route or carrying the body feet first.) The strigoi mort can resume their physical form after a week, feeding on their family as they do so, but visiting their graves everyday. They must be beheaded and their bodies burned within seven years to end their rampages. If they aren't, they're freed from the link to their grave and can spread chaos wherever they like.

The strigoi mort first returns as a form of poltergeist, wreaking havoc in their family home.

It's not just the strigoi viu that can return as strigoi mort. In some legends, simply being cruel or violent in life is enough to turn you into a strigoi, much like the fear that being vicious in life would turn you into a draugr in death (p.20). It's certainly an incentive to live an honest and kind existence. According to Ruth Owen, who writes about vampires, the living would push a silver needle through the heart of a corpse before burial to stop it from transforming into a strigoi. People might also slash tendons in the legs to stop a strigoi from walking if it returned. A more famous method involved driving an iron spike through the corpse and into the ground, usually through the heart, to pin it in place. Archaeologists sometimes encounter bodies buried in this fashion, including one skeleton that is 700 years old. Bodies might also be buried face down so if the person did turn into a strigoi, they'd dig further into the ground, and not out of their grave.

A more famous method involved driving an iron spike through the corpse and into the ground, usually through the heart, to pin it in place.

According to the Rev. Henry Fanshawe Tozer, writing in the 1860s, infants were especially targeted by the strigoi, so during a birth, anyone present would throw a stone behind them while saying "this in the mouths of the strigoi". The strigoi feed on their living family members, either by draining their energy or drinking their blood, so babies would be particularly vulnerable.

Recorded cases date back to the 1670s, but it's not a dead belief or part of forgotten folklore. Even as recently as 2004, Marotinu de Sus in southern Romania seemed to

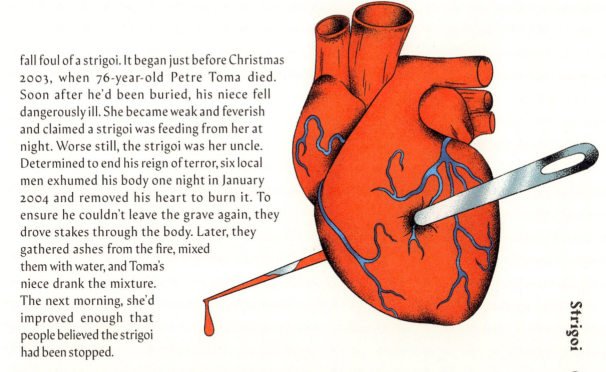

fall foul of a strigoi. It began just before Christmas 2003, when 76-year-old Petre Toma died. Soon after he'd been buried, his niece fell dangerously ill. She became weak and feverish and claimed a strigoi was feeding from her at night. Worse still, the strigoi was her uncle. Determined to end his reign of terror, six local men exhumed his body one night in January 2004 and removed his heart to burn it. To ensure he couldn't leave the grave again, they drove stakes through the body. Later, they gathered ashes from the fire, mixed them with water, and Toma's niece drank the mixture. The next morning, she'd improved enough that people believed the strigoi had been stopped.

The *Guardian* covered the story in 2005, and the sick woman was still well recovered, leading a local woman to suggest the ritual must have worked. The police arrested the men who illegally dug up the body, though they didn't serve a sentence. Locals confirmed that the ritual still occasionally takes place, but away from the watchful eye of the law. Rural communities also carry out precautions against strigoi attacks. A woman in Celaru, southern Romania, made bags containing stones, grain, an apple, a mirror, and a comb to put under the corpse's head so if they became a strigoi, believing this would enable them to lie quietly in the grave.

Far from being the glittering vampires of *Twilight* or the sexy vampires created by Anne Rice, the strigoi is an earthy, vicious spirit that only has carnage on its mind. While they're often referred to as vampires, it's perhaps more helpful to look at strigoi as troubled spirits that feed on their family. The image of the vampire has evolved so much since the 19th century that it can be difficult to categorize any spirits as vampires. Descriptions of strigoi never feature the famous fangs of Hammer Horror vampires, and they certainly don't live in castles or large houses! The strigoi appeared in sci-fi horror TV series *The Strain*, in which these parasitic monsters spread vampirism much like a virus, though the single-minded destructive nature of this version is perhaps closer to the folklore stories.

Strigoi 💀 Romania

43

SANTA COMPAÑA

You came to northern Spain to see more than the typical tourist sites. One evening, you decide to enjoy the mountain air, glad the heat has gone out of the day after sunset. You stand on the wooden verandah of your cabin and take in the view. Movement on the path below catches your eye, and a painfully gaunt man stumbles along, holding a cross aloft. The smell of candles burning drifts up to you on the evening breeze. Before you can call out a greeting, your travel companion yanks you inside and slams the sliding door. You ask her what is wrong, but she keeps her back to the door. She crosses herself and whispers "Santa Compaña"...

The Santa Compaña, or Holy Company, is a popular belief in the northwest region of Iberia, particularly in Galicia, Asturias, and northern Portugal. It refers to a procession of souls wandering through the countryside between midnight and dawn. The legend varies: the procession contains between six and twelve souls, and their purpose depends on the village. In some areas, the Santa Compaña claims the soul of someone whose death is imminent, while elsewhere, they announce whose death is coming with the year. Galician scholar Carolina Ramos explains that the conception of the procession differs slightly in each community. There is not a singular Santa Compaña, but many—as many as there are villages. In some stories, they're more common on Halloween or Midsummer's Eve, although they walk throughout the year.

The only living person in the company is the local parishioner cursed to lead the procession every night, but they wake up the next morning with no memory of what occurred. They carry a cross or holy water, and they are not allowed to look behind them at the dead following them. It's crucial that they persuade someone to take over the task so they can be released. If no one replaces them, they sicken and die within weeks, although their inability to remember their role in the procession makes it almost impossible for them to pass the task on to another. There seems to be a random element to who is chosen to lead the procession, but whether it is a man or a woman depends on which saint presides over the parish.

> **They carry a cross or holy water, and they are not allowed to look behind them at the dead following them.**

The living can't see the procession, only the living parishioner leading it, though descriptions still include the dead walking barefoot, carrying lamps, and wearing hooded cloaks. People can tell they're passing because they can smell the burning candles, or if the forest falls silent, as the animals stay still during the procession. An intense feeling of cold also accompanies them as they pass. In legend, only those accidentally baptized with the holy oil for the sick rather than holy water can see the Santa Compaña. Elsewhere, the living can only see the candles carried by the dead souls, an eerie image reminiscent of the Welsh corpse candle or Irish jack-o'-lantern.

One way to avoid the Santa Compaña is to carry a black cat or make sure your hands are full so they can't hand you a cross. You can also step away from the path, taking yourself away from the procession, and avoid looking at them as they pass. Lying on the ground and staying face down until they have passed is also an option. If these options aren't open to you, turn your hands into horns by making a fist and then raising your index and little fingers, a gesture sometimes believed to turn away the evil eye (heavy metal fans, you've done this for years). For those who feel extra ambitious, use salt or chalk to draw a Circle of Solomon and stand inside it. If you see the Santa Compaña and don't take protective measures, then you too will die within the year. But even if you do take these measures, as Ramos points out, you still won't know if your protective action helped you dodge death until a year has passed.

The stories of encounters between people and the Santa Compaña have common points. The encounter often happens late at night in an exceptionally dark place, such as a thick forest. There is only one eyewitness for each encounter and it seems groups never stumble across them, despite this area being on the route of the popular Camino de Santiago pilgrimage.

The procession is sometimes considered an Iberian equivalent of the Wild Hunt, found in Northern European folklore. It's worth remembering that the Celts lived on the Iberian peninsula during the Iron Age, so similarities with legends found further north aren't entirely surprising. That said, it's also worth viewing the Santa Compaña as its own phenomenon within its Iberian context. Unlike the Wild Hunt, often led by well-known figures like Odin, Gwyn ap Nudd or Perchta (among others), the leader of the Santa Compaña is a living person, caught up in the procession against their will. Here, we see that the dead actually need the living, in this case, to guide them in the procession. And the living need death, to keep the cycle of life going. Just make sure to keep your hands full and avert your gaze if you find yourself smelling candle wax on a lonely path in the dark...

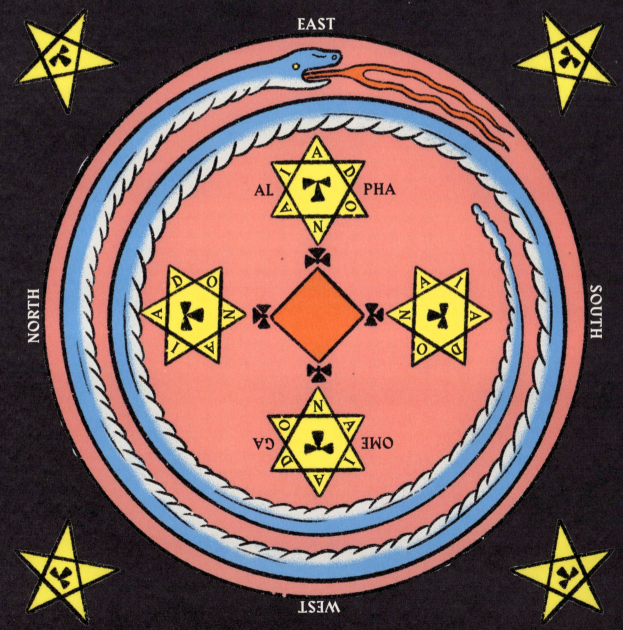

PANTAFICA

You wake suddenly, your eyes flying open in the darkness, but when you try to breathe, nothing goes in or out. Your limbs feel like they're made of concrete, pressing into the bed and refusing to move. What's going on? Why can't you move? Why can't you breathe? A wicked laugh erupts at the bottom of the bed and a dark shape hops onto the floor. The figure's cloak glows white in the sliver of moonlight falling through the curtains. Moments later, your body kicks in and you take great gulps of air. You snap on the light but you already know that the figure is gone, and that you've had a visit from Pantafica.

Pantafica is a demonic woman from Abruzzo and Marche folklore, taking the form of either an old witch dressed in white or a huge black cat. Put simply, she personifies the nightmare, because she sits on the chest of sleeping people and puts her hands (or paws) over their mouth. When she's not trying to suffocate people in their sleep, she also wanders through villages at night, braiding the manes of horses, so you can tell when she's passed. Mysterious braiding is an actual phenomenon recognized by horse owners, and in days gone by, the braids were called witches' knots, fairy knots, and elf locks. While wider folklore sees these braids as a sign your horse had been "borrowed" and ridden by fairies or witches at night, here, Pantafica is simply being mischievous—which is an improvement on trying to suffocate you.

There is a simple way to ward off Pantafica, which involves scattering sand or bags of beans near the bed. This works thanks to a long-held belief that supernatural creatures have to stop when they encounter such items and count every one. Pantafica would be so distracted by the counting that she'd leave you alone.

This phenomenon now has a medical name—sleep paralysis. It's that awful moment when you wake up, can't breathe, and can't move. People often hallucinate dark figures in the room with them at this boundary between waking and sleeping, known as hypnogogic illusions. There are some theories that the phenomenon even helps to explain alien encounters. Anywhere between 8% and 50% of people have experienced sleep paralysis, so it's unsurprising that similar figures appear across cultures. We've already seen the feline form of the draugr (p.20), crushing sleepers in the night. Pantafica appears in Brazil as Pisadeira, a witch who stomps on your stomach in the night, so you wake up breathless. Bengali folklore has the Boba, who strangles people in their sleep, while the Mokthi is the Albanian spirit who targets women in their sleep. A more generic name for the spirit is the night hag, who appears around the world. No matter what you call the creature, the experience can be truly terrifying.

Pantafica ☠ Italy

SHUBIN

You sit at the bar, transfixed as the miner beside you tells you about the time he got lost in the mine. Not because he didn't know his way around, mind you. A power cut caused the lights to fail, leaving him down there in the dark. After what felt like hours, a figure appeared carrying a lantern, and even though he didn't look quite right for a miner, and he didn't quite wear regulation safety gear, your new companion followed him to safety. You ask why he looked wrong, and the miner pauses, before admitting that in the dim light from the lantern, he could see that his rescuer wore a fur coat.

The stories of Shubin come predominantly from Ukraine's eastern Donbas region. No one can agree about the origin of the name, though one theory posits that it comes from the name for methane, shu-shu, which can build up in mines. Shubin comes in two varieties, depending on the story being told. One variety is the benevolent Shubin, who warned miners of impending disasters, and even led them to safety when required. According to the legend, Shubin is the ghost of a dead miner who had the knack of going into a mine and sensing impending danger. Miners continued to call on his predictive abilities even after he died. Variations of this story occur in several mining towns, and those miners who have experienced the same phenomenon are convinced that Shubin helped them.

Those who work in anthracite (hard coal) mines disagree, believing Shubin to be a malevolent spirit who deliberately causes accidents. In one legend, Shubin was created as part of a vicious safety test. A man arrived in Donbas looking for a job, and the miners said he could join them if he passed their test, which involved walking far into the mine with his lantern lit. If he could do this without being afraid, the job was his. Thinking it was merely a test of his mettle, the man agreed—not realizing that the miners were using him to test if there was explosive gas in the mine. He did as they asked, but died in the ensuing explosion. Shubin now haunts the mine, causing accidents that kill other miners. Shubin is believed to wear a fur coat, as the miners gave a fur coat to the man to protect his skin in case the methane in the mine caught fire.

Given the number of disasters and accidents that occur in mines, it's perhaps unsurprising that people believe them to be haunted. Cornwall, England, has its "knocker" spirits, which became the tommyknockers in the United States. Bluecaps appear in folklore along the English-Scottish border, leading miners to mineral deposits and warning of cave-ins. Yet Shubin appears as a specific ghost, linked with protective abilities or tragedy, depending on the mine. He remains a reminder of the dangers posed by working underground.

Shubin Ukraine

POLTERGEIST

It started small, with doors standing open that you thought you had closed. Your keys kept going missing or the landline would ring, and when you answered there was no one there. But now things have escalated and you can't pretend it isn't happening. Every door in your house is banging in a constant rhythm. The TV remote flies across the room, hitting the wall in an explosion of plastic. A shower of coins cascades from the ceiling in the corner, mirroring the stones falling on your roof. Every electrical appliance in your house throws out blue sparks—and you have no idea what your landlord can do about a poltergeist.

The name "poltergeist" is synonymous with violent hauntings, involving items being thrown around the room, doors slamming, or electrical items malfunctioning, among other phenomena. Whenever the term is associated with a haunting, it's clear something negative is going on. Many cases involve girls in their early teens, leading some to theorize a link between the emotional turbulence of puberty and poltergeists. Does this period of life attract these spirits, or is the activity the result of the girls' psychic powers? No one is quite sure.

The term first appears in the Erasmus Alberus dictionary of 1540 and it's made up of two German words: poltern (to create a disturbance) and geist (ghost). They were also known as a rumpelgeist, gespenst, kobold, and spectre. The range of terms used to describe the spirits can make it difficult to find accounts of them before the 19th century, when "poltergeist" became a catch-all term.

> **The name "poltergeist" is synonymous with violent hauntings, involving items thrown around the room, slamming doors, or malfunctioning electrical items, among other phenomena.**

Despite this, one of the first recorded poltergeist episodes dates to 858 CE. This account, involving a farmhouse in Bingen, Germany, came from the Annals,

Poltergeist 💀 Germany

written by a priest named Rudolf. The family living there suffered from stones being thrown (a phenomenon known as lithobolia) on the exterior walls of the house, and fires breaking out. The spirit also started arguments between the inhabitants and whipped up animosity among the local community towards one particular man. Any time he walked into a house, the spirit set fire to it, forcing the man to live in his fields since the neighbors (understandably) refused to invite him in.

The spirit even burnt the poor man's crops, and such was the ill feeling of the community towards him that he underwent a horrifying ordeal involving a hot iron to prove he was innocent. These crimes were happening around him, but he wasn't committing them himself. When he passed this awful trial, the Church sent priests from nearby Mainz to exorcize the house. The spirit reappeared after the exorcism, claiming one of the priests was under his control, and it continued its activity for three years until every building had been burned down. In Rudolf's report, this was the work of a demon, rather than a poltergeist, but later writers recognized hallmarks of poltergeist activity, such as stone-throwing and mysterious fires. The idea of the spirit speaking to people reappeared in the legend of the Bell Witch from 1800s Tennessee.

The spirit also started arguments between the inhabitants and whipped up animosity among the local community towards one particular man.

A more recent example of a German poltergeist occurred in 1967 in Rosenheim. While most stories of poltergeists involve people's homes, this one occurred in the office of a law firm. Lights flickered, objects moved by themselves, electrical appliances refused to work, the telephones rang but there was no one on the line when they were answered, and unexplained noises came from different parts of the building. Parapsychologist Hans Bender investigated the activity and noticed that the phenomena focused on 19-year-old secretary Annemarie Schneider. While Bender tried to find an explanation, perhaps related to Schneider's dislike of her job, the activity remained difficult to rationalize—although it's worth noting that it stopped when she left her job. To this day, no one can definitively explain whether the phenomena was supernatural or psychological in origin.

Historian P. G. Maxwell-Stuart explains that in the Middle Ages, the poltergeist was a ghost or demon. By the 20th century, people discussed the phenomenon as a burst of physical energy, investigated by groups like the Society for Psychical Research. This shows how slippery the term is, as it responds to the beliefs of the age.

While the poltergeist is listed here as a German spirit, thanks to its name and early accounts of their activity, stories of their chaotic outbursts occur all over Europe. The Bell Witch legend from early 1800s Tennessee and the Enfield Poltergeist phenomenon from 1970s London are two classic versions. Even further afield, the activity of the Tokoloshe spirit in South African lore is incredibly similar to that of the poltergeist. The film *Poltergeist* (1982) brought them to wider notice, and such spirits are now a mainstay of ghost-hunting TV shows and horror films.

Poltergeist 💀 Germany

CHAPTER 2

Asia & Oceania

YŪREI

Walking along a Tokyo street, you spot a small shrine amid the skyscrapers and ask your companion who it's for. She tells you of the mighty samurai Taira no Masakado, whose restless spirit disturbed the locals until a monk erected the shrine to appease it. According to legend, it was rededicated in a lavish ceremony after lightning struck a nearby building. When the Americans tried to demolish the shrine during the occupation, a series of accidents persuaded them otherwise. Such is the power, she whispers, of the yūrei.

In Japan, friends and family perform a range of rites after death and say prayers to help the soul move on to the afterlife. Once they make this journey, over time, the soul becomes a guardian of the family. People continue to honor their ancestors as family members, especially during the Obon festival in August. But without performing the proper rites, the soul gets stuck between the material and spiritual worlds. In other cases, souls can't pass on because they've died a violent or sudden death. In these situations, the soul becomes a yūrei, or "dark spirit".

Yūrei come in different varieties, and their appearance usually reflects how they died. These ghostly figures wear what they wore at the time of their death or burial, so they're often depicted in white burial kimonos. The common image of the yūrei sees them with long, tangled hair, and, as they're translucent, they appear to have no legs or feet and drift from place to place. In some depictions, the yūrei is accompanied by will-o'-the-wisps, or small flickering lights with no obvious source. The yūrei exists with a single purpose and can't move on until they're put to rest. How this happens depends on their reason for staying in this world. Finding their body and giving it a proper burial, passing on a message, or revealing their killer can all help the yūrei to rest. Priests may also exorcise them, so unlike the onryō (p.60), there are multiple ways to end a yūrei haunting. The legend of Okiku, which inspired Koji Suzuki's 1991 novel, *Ring*, tells the story of a yūrei.

Professor Koyama Satoko notes that in older times, the yūrei were simply benevolent ghosts; they've only been viewed as terrifying since the early modern period. At this point, they shifted from being a dead soul to a resentful spirit that the living must somehow appease. In the late 19th century, writer Lafcadio Hearn collected many Japanese ghost stories for Western audiences. The idea that the living must placate the dead and the dead will protect the living in return can be traced back to his work. It's important to understand that a yūrei wants something. This isn't an idle fancy, it's a soul-deep desire it needs to fulfill. Helping them to fulfill that desire also allows them to move on and find peace.

Yūrei · Japan

ONRYŌ

You lie in your bed, dozing as the evening slides towards the depths of night. The window is open, and the sounds of the city play a comforting urban lullaby. A curtain billows in a sudden gust of midnight wind, and the graceful movement reveals a figure. The white fabric becomes a burial gown, with long black hair draped across a corpse-white face. Her dark eyes glare at you, filled with menace and righteous fury. Her voice rings in your ears, issuing a curse that you cannot understand, and fear paralyses you. You didn't find this house listed on an unofficial website, the description proudly boasting haunted origins, did you? You realize it is not just a murder house, it is an onryō house. And you've come to stay.

The onryō is the yūrei you do not want to encounter (p.58). If you've seen the *Grudge* movies directed by Takashi Shimizu, then you're familiar with the concept: rage personified, infecting a place and everyone who enters it.

An onryō is all the more terrifying because they were once human. In their legend, if a person dies in the throes of hatred or rage, the soul remains stuck on earth because the emotions are so powerful. That level of fury twists the spirit, filling them with wrath, and vengeance becomes their sole motivation. As you'd imagine, many onryō are created through murder, war, or catastrophe, and they often bear a physical sign of how they died.

While onryō could simply kill their intended victims, that fate would be far too quick. They like to make the suffering last, tormenting them and everyone they hold dear for years. Onryō don't care if their actions cause collateral damage. For them, there is only fury. There is no way to bargain with them since they're so consumed with their lust for revenge. Their rage infects people and places, touching anyone who comes into contact with them. Think of the house in *Ju-On: The Grudge* (2002), in which Kayako, the resident onryō, kills anyone who sets foot inside. The final scene of the film, depicting empty Tokyo streets as missing persons posters flutter on lampposts, is a truly chilling testament to how far an onryō curse might travel.

In their legend, if a person dies in the throes of hatred or rage, the soul remains stuck on earth because the emotions are so powerful.

Onryō ☠ Japan

Not all onryō have such hateful origins, but that doesn't make them any less dangerous. A person might feel such all-consuming love for another that death contorts this passion into jealousy. They return as an onryō to haunt their lover, devastating their relationships, targeting any new children, and wreaking havoc in their lover's life. The lover left behind becomes a victim of the love they once enjoyed.

Stories of the onryō appear in writing as far back as the eighth century. An early example involves royalty: Emperor Kammu falsely accused his brother of disloyalty and consigned him to exile. His innocent brother died, and became an onryō, tormenting the emperor so much that he moved his court twice to try to escape the spirit. You can't outrun an onryō.

Onryō 💀 Japan

A person might feel such all-consuming love for another that death contorts this passion into jealousy.

They also appear in literature, most famously in the 1825 play, *Yotsuya Kaidan* (The Ghost Story of Yotsuya). While different variations of the play have been told over the years, at its core, it tells the story of Iemon, a dishonored samurai, who torments and disfigures Oiwa, his beautiful young wife. We're still familiar with her image now, with the distorted face and long black hair a fixture in Japanese horror. In some versions, Oiwa kills herself after learning of Iemon's plan to leave her for another woman, cursing Iemon as she dies. In others, Iemon murders her himself. As an onryō, Oiwa torments Iemon and his new wife. Anyone who comes into contact with them ends up dead, a point often common to onryō stories.

According to Thersa Matsuura, a writer on Japanese folklore, the 1825 play is based on a true story, and the real Oiwa died in 1636. Some even believe that the legend itself is cursed, which might explain why accidents and injuries plague productions of the story. Actors and producers visit Oiwa's grave to ask for her blessing before they mount a production of her story, sometimes leaving offerings at her shrine to appease her.

While the onryō is rightly feared, we must consider how they come into being. They're often the victim of terrible violence. This perhaps explains the strong sense of justice—and also injustice—associated with many onryō stories. Their human origins allow us to feel both terrified of and empathetic towards them. It's hardly surprising that one way to lay them to rest is to acknowledge what happened to them. Think of Sugawara no Michizane, a ninth-century politician who was exiled to a remote posting, where he died. After a period of mysterious fires, furious storms, and mass illness, a diviner realized they faced an onryō. They restored Sugawara no Michizane's official record and built a shrine to him in Kyoto, allowing the furious onryō to evolve into a revered spirit. Such is his fame today, students pray at his shrine for his help in passing exams.

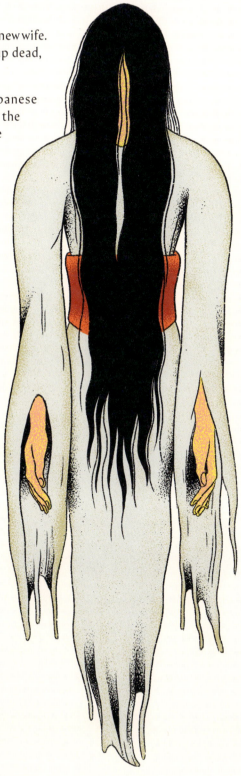

Onryō 💀 Japan

ASWANG

A peculiar "tick" sound comes from the porch and no matter how much you try to ignore it, it tickles the back of your brain. It's not quite right, though you can't say why. You fling open the door and peer out into the darkness. A woman stands outside, her long, black hair falling over her face. Something about her feet looks wrong, but you don't want to be rude. You greet her and ask if she's ok. She looks up at you and mumbles a response about a broken-down car and needing a phone. You're too busy staring into her eyes and wondering why your reflection is upside-down to hear her. Then it hits you—she's an aswang.

Aswang is the umbrella term that covers a range of monsters in Filipino folklore, including vampires, werewolves, ghouls, and witches. As a result, there is no single description to cover the aswang, especially since some accounts insist that aswang can blend in with humans when they need to. They often take human form during the day to better select the victim they will hunt when night falls. Unlike European vampires, aswang can emerge in daylight, although this is said to leave them in a weakened state. One type of aswang, the manananggal, looks like a human woman but morphs into a bat at night and feeds on fetuses. This means pregnant women are most at risk from aswang attacks, while the very sick can also be vulnerable.

> **They often take human form during the day to better select the victim they will hunt when night falls.**

In some stories, aswang marry humans, which has the unfortunate side-effect of forcing the human to become an aswang following the marriage. They're not famously social creatures though, preferring to hunt alone since they hate sharing food. Surprisingly, there are detailed instructions for how a human might have become an aswang, although it's unclear why anyone would choose this fate (and the process to switch is fairly convoluted). They'd tie a fertilized chicken egg to their stomach until the chick passed into them—the lore doesn't explain how this would happen. The human then buried the shell inside a length of bamboo with dung and coconut oil, and this transferred aswang powers to the human, though it's unclear whether the human could choose which variety of aswang they would become. Aswang could

Aswang • Philippines

also pass their abilities to a human if the aswang held their open mouth near the human's stomach. This allowed the chick inside the aswang to pass into the human's stomach, taking the aswang's powers with it.

One way to reveal whether someone is an aswang is to have albularyo in your possession, an oil made by a witch doctor. If it boils of its own accord, you're near an aswang. Much like European vampires, you can also defeat an aswang with garlic, salt, and crucifixes, although rosaries are also useful. They detest slashing sounds, so another method recommends whipping them with a stingray tail. This suggests the Buntot pagi, a whiplike weapon in the Philippines, where stingray are plentiful.

You can sometimes spot them by their bloodshot eyes or backwards-facing feet, which allow them to look like they're walking away when they're actually approaching their victims. Look into the suspected aswang's eyes—if your reflection is upside-down, then they are an aswang. Another giveaway is if the suspected figure is unable to step onto consecrated ground, regardless of the religion. People might hang special prayers over their doorway to prevent aswang from entering. It's also notable that aswang shapeshift into the form of local animals, such as bats and flying lemurs, both of which have been killed in the pursuit of aswang.

The stories first appeared in the 16th century after Spanish explorers recorded their experiences in the Philippines. These accounts suggest locals exaggerated the danger posed by aswang, although it's important to note the power dynamic at play here. Conquering nations can often dismiss local beliefs as superstitious or silly as a way to show their superiority over the people they want to colonize.

In the 1950s, the CIA even exploited local beliefs by leaving piles of dead bodies marked with aswang bites in busy areas to convince people the aswang was attacking the Huks, a guerilla organization that opposed US control over the Philippines' economy. This undermined support for the Huks until they surrendered.

One possible origin for the creature could be a rare genetic condition that causes the same kind of muscle spasms often seen in aswang depictions. Others suggest that the presence of large bats in

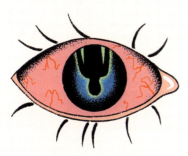
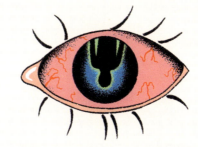

the Philippines could explain the original aswang stories. Another explanation is the appearance of similar creatures in Malaysian folklore, and Malay people took their beliefs with them when they migrated to the Philippines during the 13th century. Folklorist Maximo D. Ramos suggested aswang offered a degree of social control much like many other folkloric or ghostly figures, with parents threatening unruly children with a visit by aswang, or people claiming aswang patrolled their fields at night to deter would-be trespassers. Others suggest the Spanish invented the aswang as a monster in the forest to keep people from leaving their villages.

Look into the suspected aswang's eyes—if your reflection is upside-down, then they are an aswang.

Searching on Reddit reveals a range of accounts describing aswang encounters, both shared by the witness and those relating encounters second- or third-hand. One person described hearing an aswang walking on the roof of their home during their mother's pregnancy; try as he might, their father could never see what was making the noise. Another discussed an American professor who visited Capiz, a province in the Western Visayas region of the Philippines, as part of an exchange program and encountered an aswang that he recognized as the mayor's wife. While some accounts suggest a decrease in sightings over recent years, and others dismiss them as nothing but folklore, others insist on the genuine existence of these creatures. Perhaps it's wise to pay attention to how your reflection appears in a person's bloodshot eyes...

67

PHI HUA KHAT

You're enjoying a cup of cha yen (iced tea) in the cafe, when movement in the corner of your eye catches your attention. You glance up and notice a man walking past the window. You stare for a moment until you realize why his appearance unsettles you; he carries his head in his arms. This must be the phi hua khat you read about on the plane. Your gaze travels down and fixes on the furious expression on the ghost's face. He stalks away and a wave of relief breaks over you when he turns the corner and disappears from view. You wouldn't want to be the person he's looking for.

Specialist in Thai folklore, Phya Anuman Rajathon, explains that before the 12th century, the phi were spirits that were part of the local animistic practices, and were divided into both good and bad phi. Following the arrival of both Brahmanism and Buddhism, the good phi became recognized as gods, while the bad phi became evil spirits or ghosts. Even today, phi is the Thai word for ghost, particularly evil spirits or the ghosts of those who either died under awful circumstances or who suffered a lot in life. The phi hua khat is a ghost rather than an evil spirit, and is someone who died from sudden decapitation. Carrying his own head, people consider him angry and dangerous. Full of resentment from his death, he terrorizes those he encounters, and he is also sometimes blamed for outbreaks of unexplained disease.

Some believe the phi hua khat can be traced back to the use of beheading as a form of execution. This perhaps explains why a special ceremony was introduced during executions to ensure the condemned man didn't return as a phi hua khat, as described by American painter P. A. Thompson, who recounted seeing one such public execution in the early 19th century. Monks preached to the prisoner, who was often given opium before being tied to a cross made from bamboo. The executioner filled the prisoner's ears with clay and handed him lit joss sticks. One executioner distracted the prisoner while the other performed an elaborate sword dance before making his killing blow. The body would be buried, while the head was mounted on a pole as a warning to others. People believed that performing this ritual stopped the prisoner's ghost from returning as a phi hua khat after death. Firing squads eventually replaced beheading as the method of execution in the 20th century.

Unlike other ghosts in this volume, there are few practices to deter a phi hua khat, which perhaps reflects how rare they have become since the method of public execution changed. But people may still consult a phi doctor if a dangerous spirit needs to be contained, whether that is a phi hua khat or another type of phi. The phi doctor is a specialist in dealing with ghosts, and can bind the malevolent phi inside an earthenware jar which is sealed and dumped into a deep lake to prevent its escape.

JIĀNGSHĪ

You hide behind the tree on the forest's edge and listen hard. Somewhere off to your right, a twig snaps. You hold your breath and peer into the gloom. There is a figure lumbering around in the undergrowth, its unearthly, jerky movements giving away its location. It wears a long blue robe and its pale skin shimmers in the pre-dawn light, its fingers twisted into savage claws. It's a jiāngshī and it has followed you ever since you got too close to the cave, looking for shelter in the dark. Moments later, a cock crows on the nearby farm and the jiāngshī unleashes a frustrated cry. It hops back into the forest, towards the cave, while you head to the road. That was close. Too close.

The jiāngshī, or "Stiff Corpse", is known as the Chinese hopping vampire because of its jumping movements, caused by stiffened limbs due to rigor mortis. They first appeared in literature during the Qing Dynasty (1644–1911), and are usually depicted as a stiff corpse dressed in Qing dynasty-era clothing. Specifically, they first appear in a range of reflections by Ji Xiaolan who was the first to describe them in his 1800 work, Yuewei Caotang Biji (Random Notes at the Cottage of Close Scrutiny). Sometimes they look like regular people, but others have decomposed further if they've been dead longer. Other jiāngshī have long nails, fangs, and give off a green glow.

"Vampire" is a bit of a misnomer, because the traditional jiāngshī doesn't drink blood or turn into a bat. Instead, it feeds on a person's qi (life force) or their flesh, making them closer to a zombie. Feeding on qi both sustains them and allows them to grow in power; the jiāngshī can even gain the power of flight if enough years pass. More contemporary depictions sometimes see them drink blood, thanks to Western influences.

> **Sometimes they look like regular people, but others have decomposed further if they've been dead longer. Other jiāngshī have long nails, fangs, and give off a green glow.**

Jiāngshī ☠ China

71

There are a range of ways to become a jiāngshī. A person might not be buried according to the proper rites, or not buried at all. In this case, the body gets restless and returns to the living, even though it cannot rejoin them. They might have suffered a violent death, or be resurrected by a magical practitioner. A corpse might absorb too much yang qi (the energy that drives biological functions) or not decompose properly, also leading them to become a jiāngshī. Or their soul might remain in the body, especially if they died suddenly or at their own hand. If the corpse was hit by lightning, or a cat leapt over the body, the corpse might return as a jiāngshī. A person might even be transformed into a jiāngshī if they're bitten or scratched by one.

Thankfully, they have a whole range of weaknesses if you find yourself face-to-face with one. You could stop a jiāngshī in its tracks by showing it its reflection, especially in an eight-sided bagua mirror, or by pinning a talisman to its forehead. You could treat string with chicken blood, burnt talismans, and black ink, and use this to tie up a jiāngshī. They hate peach wood, so priests might fight them off with wooden swords made of peach, and they despise cockerels, no doubt because their cry heralds sunrise. Or you can drop a bag of coins and the jiāngshī will stop to count them, reflecting the "counting" countermeasure that also wards off Pantafica (p.48). Even holding your breath could save you, as it leaves the jiāngshī unable to locate you. But the simplest solution? Many tales advise avoiding them at all costs.

...they despise cockerels, no doubt because their cry heralds sunrise.

Some think the jiāngshī dates to earlier centuries when travel across great distances was much more difficult. People sought work in large cities, but when they died, their families worried their souls would be homesick. They might hire a priest to resurrect the corpse and lead them home so they could be buried in the family grave.

Jiāngshī 💀 China

The priests made talismans by writing in vermillion ink on yellow paper, which they attached to the corpse's forehead, so the priest could both resurrect and control the corpse. The priests and their unusual companions traveled on minor roads by night, ringing bells to warn of their approach since it was bad luck for people to see a jiāngshī.

Another theory is more mundane and references the practice of "corpse-driving". Here, families paid corpse-drivers to bring the bodies of their deceased loved ones home. The corpse-drivers placed bamboo poles under the armpits of the dead to transport them. Those carrying the poles held them on their shoulders, so the corpses looked like they were hopping. They traveled at night to avoid crowds, further adding to the mystique around the jiāngshī. It could also explain why the jiāngshī are associated with nocturnal activity, hiding in caves or coffins during the day.

They've appeared in many Hong Kong films in the 1980s and 1990s, where their jerky movements are sometimes played for comedy. *Mr Vampire* from 1985 is perhaps the best known, offering a combination of action, horror, and slapstick. Their Qing Dynasty clothing makes them recognizable when they appear in video games, even influencing the design of the Pionpi baddies in Super Mario Land. While their origins lie within a specific historical context, their stories retain enough unique details for vampire and zombie fans to find them fascinating today.

YUAN GUI

The night grows quieter as you walk down darker streets away from the bright lights and bustle of the main shopping district. Now you can hear animals rustling in rubbish bins, or snippets of conversation as you pass open windows. A giggle here, a burst of a TV jingle there; it seems that life continues everywhere you look. Suddenly, a low wailing coming from an alley to your right makes you pause. Is someone in trouble? Does someone need help? Or is that just an animal? You peer into the gloom, straining to see the source. A gray figure detaches itself from the shadows and drifts towards you, a translucent man with sad eyes and his hands balled into fists. He ignores your questions and unleashes another wail, only stopping when you turn to walk away. He stares into your face and begs you to find out what happened to him before he fades from view.

This kind of spirit is a Yuan Gui. The name translates as "ghost with grievance", which gives us a clue about what drives this Chinese spirit. The stories of the Yuan Gui were recorded as far back as the Zhou Dynasty (1046 BCE–256 BCE) in the Zuo Zhuan, a text of ancient Chinese history.

Yuan Gui are the ghosts of people who died a wrongful, cruel, or unjust death—a common reason for spirits becoming "stuck" on earth in many cultures. In some stories, they die having been wrongfully accused of something, leaving a stain on their reputation. Yet in others, they don't know why they died. As a troubled soul, Yuan Gui can't find peace, meaning they can't move on to their next life. This keeps them trapped in this world, restless and frustrated. They may take out their resentment on the living or seek revenge for their deaths, although they're not as dangerous as Japan's onryō (p.60). If anything, Yuan Gui simply want to find peace.

Sometimes Yuan Gui might contact the living to ask for their help, since they can't solve the mystery around their death on their own. They may prompt the living to investigate their death to uncover what happened, and this new information can help the troubled soul finally find peace. Alternatively, the living can help them clear their name, again to help them find peace. The living might also help them to finish any outstanding business so the Yuan Gui can gain a sense of closure and move on.

While some ghosts have a distinctive appearance that makes them easy to spot, the best way to recognize a Yuan Gui is its plaintive cry for help in the night. Unlike some of the other ghosts in this volume, there is no list of precautions to ward off a Yuan Gui. Helping them to find justice or restore their honor is the best way to appease them since this allows them to move on and not bother you—or anyone else—again.

NAALE BAA

You're brushing your teeth when you first hear it. Tap tap tap. What's that? Is someone at the door? At this time of night? You glance at the clock—midnight. Tap tap tap. This can't be good news so late. You open the app for your video doorbell to see who's calling, only the doorstep is empty. Tap tap tap. Except someone is still knocking at the door. You whisper "Naale Baa" and stare at the camera feed. Whoever it is has stopped knocking... for now.

According to one version of this legend, a female ghost walked the streets of the Maleshawaram village in Bangalore at midnight, knocking on doors. She would knock several times but move on if you didn't open the door. But if you did answer her knock, she'd possess you. One backstory for this version of the legend suggested the ghost was once a bride whose groom died before they could marry. She began searching for him, which explains all the door-knocking. In other variations, she was a witch. She only knocked on the doors of homes where men lived, mimicking the voices of their mothers, sisters, or wives to entice them to come outside. If he did so, the witch either killed him on the spot, or within the next 24 hours. In other versions, the ghost (or witch) only visited on a full moon. In one variation, she transformed men into sheep rather than killing them. People who wanted to avoid the curse wrote Naale Baa on their door, or "come tomorrow". They might utter the words if the witch knocked on the door, which turned her away. When she returned the next day, she'd see the phrase again, and move on. It's important to note that the statement was designed to turn her away respectfully so as not to enrage the witch, rather than defeat her. Eventually, people in the village stopped reporting visits by the witch, suggesting that she either moved on or faded away.

The legend enjoyed its heyday in the early 1990s, although the legend also circulated in the late 1960s and early 1970s. While it's unclear where it originated, one theory sees the story used as a pretext to encourage people to stay inside and keep their doors closed so criminals could work undetected outside. Another theory dates the story to the 1920s, when a plague epidemic swept through the area. Locals wrote the phrase on the door to ward off plague-carrying rats.

While other folk tales often offer a cautionary lesson, the moral of this story is a little harder to spot at first. Not opening the door at night could keep you safe from those who wish you harm, but it also cuts you off from your community. Yet the Naale Baa writing provides a way to ward off the potential danger so that you could remain available to friends and neighbors. Unless, of course, the ghost ever decided to ignore the Naale Baa instruction and just keep knocking...

IFRIT

The video pops up on your social media feed, suggested by the algorithm, showing the impressive sight of a desert dust devil. You've only seen them in films before, but seeing this one rage along the edge of a small town puts Hollywood to shame. Whoever films the video through a hotel window points out its height, but you're too busy staring at the images to take in what they're saying. The dust devil dwarfs the buildings it dances past, and just as the video ends, you could have sworn you saw a giant form, all wings and horns and claws, in the sand.

The ifrit, also spelled as afreet or afrit, is a demonic spirit linked with the underworld. The ifrit appears in the Qur'an. In Islamic culture, they're part of the class of supernatural beings called jinn, but for some writers, they also appear in wider folklore where the term designates a specific type of demon. They're made of smokeless fire, sometimes depicted with wings, horns, fangs, multiple heads, or claws, although they can also appear in other forms, like animals and humans. However they appear, they are considered the most evil of the jinn.

In Egypt, the ifrit is sometimes linked with spirits of the dead, and wanders cemeteries or places the deceased visited. Rabia Chaudhury, who makes podcasts about the jinn, notes the belief that those who died unnatural deaths might become an ifrit. The worry that the dead might become a powerful, vengeful spirit is a concern we see with other supernatural beings like the onryō (p.60). If a murdered person did return as an ifrit, the ifrit might avenge their death.

They're made of smokeless fire, sometimes depicted with wings, horns, fangs, multiple heads, or claws...

Other legends claim the ifrit doesn't come from a murdered person, but rather from a murder victim's blood. Having willed themselves into being, they could take on different forms, including that of the victim, a sandstorm, or the Devil. Dr Ali Olomi, a historian of Middle Eastern and Islamic history, notes that some people believe ifrits cause dust devils or sandstorms. In other legends, the ifrit is drawn to the blood, and they derive power from it, rather than emerging from the blood. Since they draw power from this blood, it leaves them with a desire to avenge the victim.

Ifrit • Persia and Egypt

According to some sources, there were ifrit sightings in Egypt in the early 20th century and British soldiers were warned not to follow any strange dogs since they might be an ifrit trying to lead them into the desert. The ifrit posed a danger to humans because they might possess a person, either in full or only possessing a single limb, and while the individual would gain inhuman strength during the possession, the ifrit would also drive them mad. Sometimes, they're more of a trickster than a downright malevolent being, stealing valuable items, or taking the form of beautiful people to seduce humans.

Ifrits often live in ruins, abandoned places or temples, organizing themselves in social hierarchies that humans would recognize, with rulers or even kings. They're both strong and cunning, and they're also incredibly fast when they move, traveling great distances at speed. While they usually marry each other, some stories speak of marriages between ifrits and humans. Ifrits are usually malevolent in their actions, although while they're immune to human weapons and can shapeshift or cast spells, ifrits are still vulnerable to magic being used against them. Sorcerers can summon or compel them, most famously binding them to objects to neutralize them or force the ifrit to use their abilities in service of the sorcerer. King Solomon himself was even believed to have encountered an ifrit, who offered to transport the Queen of Sheba's throne for him. Trying to work with an ifrit is considered black magic and best avoided for your own safety.

In the famous collection of Middle Eastern folk stories, *One Thousand and One Nights*, the beings bound in magical bottles are ifrits—which might make you

Ifrit 💀 Persia and Egypt

look at Aladdin's friendly genie a little differently. In one story in *One Thousand and One Nights*, a fisherman accidentally catches a jar containing an ifrit who swears to kill him. As a last boon before death, the clever fisherman asks the ifrit how he managed to fit into the jar. When the ifrit climbs back into the jar to show him, the fisherman replaces the stopper. The ifrit buys his freedom by telling the fisherman how to become rich.

Sorcerers can summon or compel them, most famously binding them to objects to neutralize them.

The ifrit has also made the move into other forms of media, from books and TV shows to video games. An ifrit appears in *American Gods* as a taxi driver in New York, where he can be recognized by his flaming eyes. Meanwhile, the ifrit is a recurring summon in the *Final Fantasy* games, dealing fire-elemental damage, while also appearing as a fire-resistant creature in *Dungeons & Dragons*.

FISHER'S GHOST

A full moon lights your way along the dirt path, and the bridge looms up ahead. You walk faster, hurrying to get home, when you realize someone is sitting on the rail on one side of the bridge. It's a man dressed in old-fashioned clothing, although he seems luminescent in the gloom. He turns to look at you, revealing a gaping head wound that oozes blood down his forehead. Before you can ask if he needs help, he raises one arm and points along the narrow dribble of a creek. He lowers his head and disappears, still pointing.

This early 19th-century story of Fisher's Ghost takes us to Campbelltown, New South Wales. The once-rural town has since been swallowed up by Sydney.

As the legend goes, Frederick Fisher, our eponymous ghost, was born in London but ended up in Australia as a convict, when he was shipped across the world as a punishment for his crime. Having completed his sentence, he acquired land and began working as a farmer. He disappeared from Campbelltown on June 17 1826. Soon after, his neighbor George Worrell announced Fisher hadn't disappeared; he'd returned to London. Before leaving, Fisher granted him power of attorney over his farm.

There is a nugget of truth to the story in that Fisher signed his Australian property to Worrell when facing arrest again for pulling a knife on someone, although problems began when Fisher left prison. When he returned to his farm, Worrell claimed the land to be his. Fisher disappeared and Worrell again took over the farm, claiming Fisher had returned to England to avoid another arrest. People grew suspicious, since Worrell started wearing Fisher's clothes and sold his horse.

People may invent ghosts like these to reveal information, or to point the finger of blame without recrimination.

Police arrested Worrell for Fisher's murder, and Worrell accused four other men. Two boys crossed Fisher's land while taking a shortcut and spotted bloodstains.

They also found hair and a tooth. A constable found nothing, but hired an Indigenous tracker who confirmed human remains in the area. Once Fisher's remains were found, Worrall was tried in court. According to legend, he confessed before he was hanged, claiming it was a mistake, although few believed his version of events. Fisher's remains were re-buried in a Campbelltown cemetery in a grave without a headstone.

Yet this is not the version most people know. In the more famous variation of the legend, a local man, John Farley, claimed he'd seen Fisher's ghost sitting on a bridge shortly after Fisher's disappearance. He knew it was a ghost because the figure glowed and dripped blood from a horrific head wound. Farley insisted the ghost pointed to a field and vanished. This was the field which, when searched, revealed Fisher's remains.

Some theories suggest Farley knew where Fisher's body was, but couldn't reveal the location without implicating himself. Inventing the ghost gave him an excuse to point police in the right direction. It's worth noting the ghost does not appear in any contemporary police records.

Two boys crossed Fisher's land while taking a shortcut and spotted bloodstains. They also found hair and a tooth.

Fisher's Ghost has been described as Australia's most famous ghost (which is surprising given there have been multiple spectral appearances of opera singer Frederick Federici at Melbourne's Princess Theatre over the years). Even Charles Dickens published a retelling of the story in his Household Words magazine in 1853, while magician John Pepper used it as the basis of his "Pepper's Ghost" illusion in Sydney.

According to Campbelltown City Council, locals think Fisher's ghost still haunts the Campbelltown Town Hall. But Fisher's ghost is not a recurring ghost, like the green lady ghost of Stirling Castle (p.36); instead, it provides an example of a ghost that posthomously helps the living solve its murder, or a "crime-solving ghost". Here, the ghost becomes part of an investigation, imparting information or revealing clues, much like the ghost encountered by Athenodorous (p.18). Most commonly, the ghost reveals the location of its body, especially in tales of a disappearance. People may invent ghosts like these to reveal information, or to point the finger of blame without recrimination. This was a recurring story motif throughout the Victorian period, tying together the popular interest in the supernatural with the growing interest in detective fiction. The story can also be classified as a supernatural legend, which is a story presented as being factual that apparently validates a folk tale.

Writer Joe Nickell suggests the story of the ghost was never true, and that even Farley's supposed deathbed confirmation of the sighting was invented to support the story rather than the truth. A whole array of dubious stories try to explain the "ghost", from an ex-convict wearing a special cloak so he could expose Fisher's location while remaining anonymous, to the tale being a journalist's hoax that was re-presented as being true.

The area still celebrates the Festival of Fisher's Ghost, which began in 1956. People have even held vigils at midnight on June 17 on the bridge where Farley claimed to see Fisher. While the bridge is no longer in the same place, and indeed the original accounts have Fisher sitting on a fence, not a bridge, people still hope to see Fisher's Ghost.

GWISIN

You follow your companion into the abandoned building, careful to avoid the broken glass still stuck in the window frame. Inside, the floor is dusty. Footprints trace the routes taken by earlier urban explorers, disappearing down the corridors into the gloom. Flicking on your head torch, you creep along the passage towards a pair of double doors, passing broken furniture and faded posters on the peeling walls. Your friend disappears through the swinging doors and leaves you alone in the corridor. Suddenly, you hear something behind you—barely a whisper, but enough to catch your attention. You turn, and see a young woman floating in mid-air several yards away. Her long, black hair drifts around her body, which is clad in a white gown. You swear, wishing your friend would return. They told you how to deal with security guards, but not a gwisin.

The gwisin is a Korean ghost, a form of restless spirit created when a person dies leaving unfinished business. That may be a benevolent purpose, like looking after their family, or it could be a dangerous purpose, like seeking revenge. The gwisin stays on earth until it completes its business, and then may finally go to the underworld. Korean shamanism influences gwisin belief, and shamans suggest appeasing the ghosts so they can pass over into the afterlife.

Gwisin are a common form of ghost and people often use tales of them to scare each other. Researcher Sunhee Jun notes that the boundary between good and evil is unclear regarding the gwisin; it's such a broad category involving different types of spirit. For the most part, the gwisin is transparent, and seems to have no legs, meaning it appears to float in the air towards you.

> **The gwisin stays on earth until it completes its business, and then may finally go to the underworld.**

There are different types of gwisin, depending on the circumstances involving the individual. The cheonyeo gwisin is perhaps the most recognizable type of gwisin, with her white mourning gown and long, loose, black hair. She wears her hair this way since only married women were allowed to wear their hair up. Since a woman's purpose in earlier times was to marry and have a family, those women who didn't do

so became the cheonyeo gwisin when they died. In some tales, they're particularly found in abandoned buildings or forests—basically, anywhere humans don't live.

They're often considered malevolent and, in an interesting twist, some folklore suggests villages warded off these ghosts with phallic statues in earlier centuries. K-horror fans will recognize this type of ghost from *Whispering Corridors* (1998) and *Phone* (2002), although the cheonyeo gwisin also resembles the female onryō from J-horror films like *Ringu* (1998) and *Ju-On: The Grudge* (2002).

Surprisingly, the cheonyeo gwisin has a male counterpart, the chonggak gwisin, or bachelor ghost. They're rarely shown in films, perhaps because there's more of a market for female rage in cinema. In folklore, people might conduct rituals to play matchmaker between the cheonyeo gwisin and chonggak gwisin. The ghosts might choose to marry, even after death, and with their life purpose now complete, they can move on from the world of the living (if only all ghost hauntings were solved with such sweet matrimony!).

There is also a mul gwisin, which is the ghost of a person who drowned. The ghosts are stuck in the water where they died, so if the living get too close, they may try to drag a swimmer into the depths to join them. Some believe the mul gwisin thinks they're still alive, and they cling to the living looking for help, not intending to drown them. Either way, this ghost acts as a cautionary tale, to take care while swimming.

The dalgyal gwisin, or egg ghost, is perhaps the most unsettling of all. It has no limbs or face, appearing as an egg, and seeing one is supposed to foretell your death. This is the most inscrutable of the ghosts, with no apparent emotions or even character. No one knows the origin of this eerie spirit, although, in some legends, it haunts lonely mountain paths. There are some downright uncanny depictions of the dalgyal gwisin online, depicting humans with no faces; only a smooth, egg-like surface where the face should be. In some folklore, the dalgyal gwisin takes the form of an egg so that it can hide from the living until it chooses to appear in front of an individual.

While some attest that an encounter with a dalgyal gwisin heralds your imminent death, the fact that accounts of such encounters exist suggests that survival must be possible. In other lore, they were people who died without descendants, and they lost their humanity since they had no one to honor them. Another legend suggests the dalgyal gwisin lived and died alone, so no human essence remained after their death. Despite how terrifying this ghost sounds, knowing they lived such a solitary life also makes them seem incredibly sad, and reminds us of the importance of community.

The ghosts might choose to marry, even after death, and with their life purpose now complete, they can move on from the world of the living.

Gwisin 💀 Korea

PRETA

Your host family takes you to the park, where hundreds of people from the neighborhood cluster around small fires in metal containers. The air is thick with celebration and joy, and people leave piles of food on small altars nearby. Everyone in your group drops paper cutouts of cars, cellphones, and mansions into the fire, cheering as sparks and small curls of burnt paper flutter into the night air. Hopefully the hungry ghosts will enjoy the offering as much as the family enjoys making it.

The preta is a wandering spirit that appears in Hinduism, Taoism, and Buddhism. The name comes from the Sanskrit word preta, which means "departed" or "deceased". Originally, it referred to any ghost, but Buddhism adopted it to refer to a specific type of ghost—the hungry ghost, or preta.

While some accounts suggest pretas are largely invisible to the living, others offer visual descriptions of different types of preta. Some are naked, while others are covered in hair, and yet more dress in rags. Their ribs and veins stand out beneath their skin, and a foul smell accompanies them. Pretas are often depicted with thin necks and limbs but distended stomachs, which, despite their size, are perpetually empty, highlighting their continual starvation. Some have throats so narrow they can't swallow anything, while others have mouths so tiny they can't open them enough to fit food inside. Others can't find food at all, and some pretas even have creatures living on them that gnaw on their flesh.

> **Pretas are often depicted with thin necks and limbs but distended stomachs, which, despite their size, are perpetually empty, highlighting their continual starvation.**

The preta's punishment is to feel constant hunger they can't satisfy, although some pretas end up with cravings for abject things like corpses, feces, or mucus. Pretas remain restless in death, tortured by thirst and hunger, and they wander aimlessly in search of sustenance. One legend tells of a preta doomed to eat his own flesh. In life, he'd been a merchant who cheated his customers and unlawfully seized their property. Religious advisors suggested he change his ways, so he told them to eat their own flesh. After death, his insult to the advisors became his eternal curse.

In Buddhism, being too possessive or materialistic in life could lead to becoming a preta after death, since these actions in life affect the person's karma (what happens to a person is the result of the good or bad actions that person takes in life). This leads to them being reborn in the realm of the hungry ghosts. Here, an over-emphasis on meeting material needs ignores spiritual needs, creating a void that can never be filled with things they can buy. You might think of Tyler Durden's famous "you are not your khakis" speech in *Fight Club* (1999) or Renton's "Choose Life" speech from *Trainspotting* (1996) for contemporary riffs on this ancient theme. This insatiable lust for material goods makes the preta pitiable rather than terrifying, and they're often more of a nuisance. People try to comfort them, rather than exorcise them.

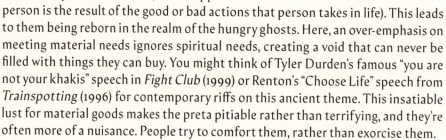

One of the more famous ways to do this is part of the Zhong Yuan Jie, or Hungry Ghost Festival, which falls on the 15th night of the seventh month of the Chinese calendar. It is believed that during this time, ghosts can leave hell for a month to be among the living. As a result, it has become common to leave offerings of food or to burn joss sticks and paper representations of money, cars, or expensive consumer goods. These items help to satiate the desires of the materialistic spirits. Over time, the paper items that are burned have changed to better reflect the preoccupations of the time: by the mid-20th century, people began burning images of shoes, toothbrushes, or even medicine. During the Covid pandemic, people burned paper vaccines.

This insatiable lust for material goods makes the preta pitiable rather than terrifying, and they're often more of a nuisance.

Preta · East Asia

In Singapore, people also hold dinners in their neighborhoods and offer rice, fruit, oil, and sugarcane to the hungry ghosts. In Malaysia, Indonesia, and Singapore, people erect stages and mount live performances, with the front row reserved for hungry ghosts. Japanese Buddhists make offerings called segaki to ease the preta's suffering in mid-August, often during the Obon festival of the dead. In some parts of China, people might offer prayers alongside traditional items and float lanterns on local rivers as part of the festivities.

Despite the efforts to comfort the preta with these rites, people also try to avoid getting their attention by not going out after dark, standing on roadside offerings, or peering under altar tables. Any of these things might provoke a hungry ghost into action. You can also avoid wearing red or black, which attracts ghosts, or even cutting your hair. People try to avoid getting married or moving house during the seventh lunar month since this may also attract a preta's attention.

Various ghosts in this volume may be scary yet somehow empathetic, like the onryō (p.60), created through an act of unspeakable cruelty, or the Yuan Gui (p.74), unable to rest until justice is done. Yet the preta seems uncomfortably familiar, created as they are through their lust in life for material goods or their use of harsh words against others. Easing their suffering is an act of kindness, but it's also a good reminder to the living to re-evaluate their priorities.

THE NIGHT MARCHERS

The house party is in full swing, with people huddling together to shout over the music, or dancing in the living room. A small group takes refuge in the kitchen, bonding over shared interests. You join this group until a loud sound cuts through the hubbub in the house. Was it a trumpet, or a horn of some kind? Your host turns pale and explains it is a conch shell announcing the approach of the Night Marchers. She draws the blinds and locks the door, ushering you all to the other side of the kitchen. You all try not to look at the window, but you can't help sneaking a glance at the bouncing torchlight passing along the road outside.

The huaka'i pō is the legendary Hawaiian procession of ghostly warriors also known as the Night Marchers, with huaka'i meaning a parade or procession, and pō meaning night. In some legends, Hawaiian deities march in their midst. According to popular folklore, if you cross the path of the Night Marchers, they'll kill you and you'll become part of their procession.

The Night Marchers are bands of phantom warriors escorting the ghosts of Hawai'i's ali'i (chiefs) in a procession to the sacred grounds. They march across the islands, and petroglyphs on the Big Island are believed to depict the Night Marchers, which would mean they pre-date the Hawaiian Kingdom (1795–1893). People have reported seeing torches in the parts of the jungle that are so dense there are no trails. Other reported sightings include phantom warriors marching behind torchbearers, or people hearing drumming or the blowing of conch shells.

> **According to popular folklore, if you cross the path of the Night Marchers, they'll kill you and you'll become part of their procession.**

The procession traces to a belief that the ali'i were descended from gods and their mana (power) must be preserved. One way to preserve this mana was to avoid

The Night Marchers   Hawai'i

interactions with ordinary people. Interactions could include a person seeing an aliʻi or having the aliʻi's shadow fall on them, which helps to explain why the processions took place at night, so ordinary people wouldn't come into contact with the aliʻi when they traveled to sacred grounds. This wasn't just for the benefit of the aliʻi; if an ordinary person made eye contact with an aliʻi, it broke a kapu (taboo), meaning the person would be put to death.

The warriors also played drums or conch shells to let people know the aliʻi were on their way. These alerts gave people time to stop their tasks and leave the area. Alternatively, people bowed and kept their gaze fixed firmly on the ground as the procession passed so they didn't see any aliʻi or touch the procession's shadows.

The Night Marchers are believed to appear during Pō Kāne, or the Night of Kāne, which is the 27th night of the lunar month, named for the god Kāne. No one is entirely sure why they chose this night for their processions, though Hawaiian writer and podcaster Kamuela Kaneshiro suggests the waning moon gave the aliʻi enough light to perform their tasks at the sacred grounds while casting smaller shadows. This meant fewer people were likely to see them, or their shadows, thus preserving their mana.

One of Kaneshiro's ancestors, Chief Kaʻiana, is thought to be in the procession due to his status. While on a ghost investigation with the Hawaiʻi Ghost Hunter's Society, members joked that Kaneshiro's lineage would prove useful should they encounter the Night Marchers, since he would be spared as a descendant of Chief Kaʻiana. Kaneshiro reports having encountered the Night Marchers twice, both hearing a conch shell blown through the night and seeing what looked like the procession.

While the Night Marchers will walk through anything that stands in their way, they will avoid the Ti plant, or Cordyline fruticosa, since it is sacred to the god Lono. You can plant Ti to help redirect the Night Marchers' route. If your front door and back door line up, your home may end up on the Night Marchers' route, so planting Ti plants outside would help.

The Night Marchers 💀 Hawaiʻi

96

If you hear them coming while you're outside, it's best to run. But if you don't have time to escape, then you have two options. If you know your lineage, you should lie on the ground, cover your head, and chant your lineage. Any ancestors among the Night Marchers might recognize you as a descendant, and they'll shout "Na'u", or "Mine!" and the procession will pass you by. If your attempts to placate them go awry, you'll hear a cry of "O-ia!", or "Let him be pierced", and you will meet your end. For anyone without ancestors among the Night Marchers, play dead or refuse to look at them. If you're indoors when you hear the Night Marchers, simply stay inside and don't look out of the windows.

While the Night Marchers will walk through anything that stands in their way, they will avoid the Ti plant, or Cordyline fruticosa, since it is sacred to the god Lono.

While some of the processional etiquette recalls that of the Santa Compaña (p.44), the lore surrounding the Night Marchers grew out of Hawai'i's Indigenous religion and beliefs. It's worth bearing in mind that the rituals are as much for the onlooker's benefit as the Night Marchers themselves. Just remember the punishment for breaking a kapu, like looking at an ali'i, was death...

The Night Marchers Hawai'i

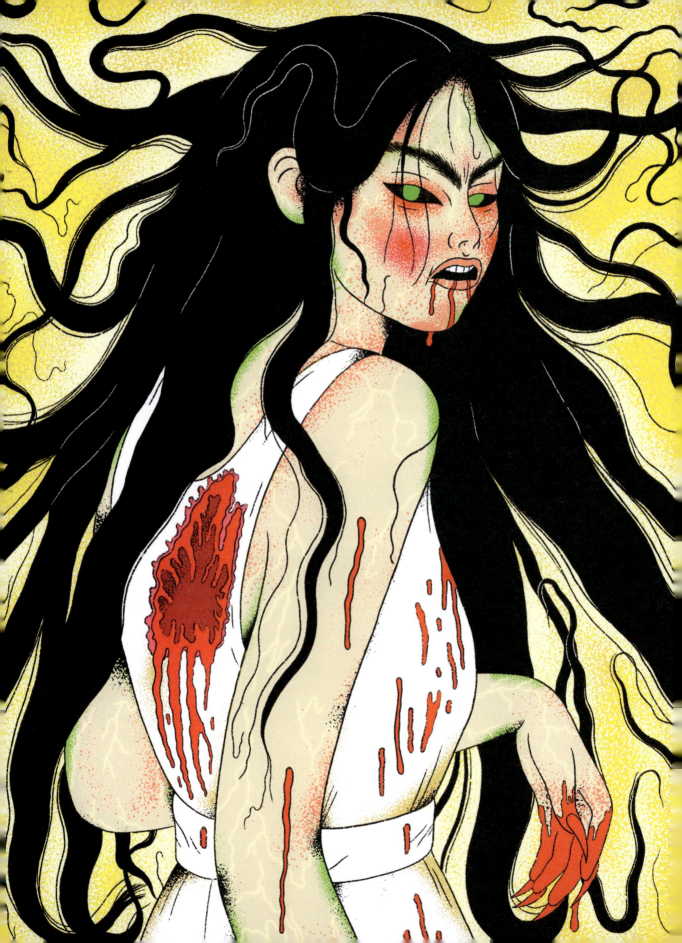

SUNDEL BOLONG

You sit at the bar, watching the woman in white standing by the jukebox flirt with a man dressed like a tourist. You can't hear their conversation but you watch her stroke his arm and laugh when he speaks. He grins like a cat that won a year's supply of cream. When she gestures to the door, he nods enthusiastically. His friends don't seem to notice that he's leaving, and he only has eyes for the woman. A gust of wind parts her long hair as they head out of the door and you spot the gaping hole in her back. Something dark red glistens inside the void.

The sundel bolong is a vengeful female ghost in Indonesian mythology and Javanese folklore, notable for her luxurious long hair and traditional white Javanese gown. According to legend, a sundel bolong was created when an unmarried woman died while pregnant or during childbirth. She's known for the large hole in her back, formed by giving birth in the grave, which is hidden by her hair. She's also usually referred to as a sex worker thanks to her name; sundel often translates to "prostitute", while bolong translates to "hole". Stories often revel in grotesque descriptions of her internal organs visible through the orifice.

If the man refuses her advances, she will castrate him, sometimes using her own fingernails.

This angry spirit is dangerous to men and children, stealing the latter to replace her own, though it's unclear what becomes of them once she snatches them. Newborns are especially vulnerable, reminding her of her lost child, while she uses her beautiful hair to catch the attention of men. In some versions of the story, the sundel bolong can shapeshift, luring men away from crowded places in the form of animals or as a beautiful woman, before resuming her monstrous form. In other versions, the sundel bolong frightens any man that sees her, prompting him to run away to safety. Other versions still see the sundel bolong portrayed as so attractive to men that they find it hard to resist her offer to leave with her. It's difficult to find information about what happens if a man does accompany the Sundel Bolong, though some stories suggest she will drain their life force. If the man refuses her advances, she will castrate him, sometimes using her own fingernails.

Variations in the legend exist depending on the region in which the story was collected. While the version in which she died during pregnancy seems the most common, some stories portray the sundel bolong as a woman murdered by people close to her. Much like the onryō (p.60), the violence and betrayal inherent in the killing keeps the ghost tied to the world of the living and provides a motivation for her thirst for vengeance. In these stories, the sundel bolong's very existence reminds us of a great wrong enacted against her; the ghost would not exist were it not for the awful betrayal.

> **...the violence and betrayal inherent in the killing keeps the ghost tied to the world of the living and provides a motivation for her thirst for vengeance.**

There is a suggestion that the myth was a cautionary tale told to Europeans to warn men off visiting local sex workers during the 1600s, when the Dutch East India Company occupied Indonesia. Similar figures exist in southeast Asia, with the pontianak in Malaysia, the langsuyar in Bali, and the kuntilanak in Indonesia—also countries that have suffered as a result of colonialism. The figures share a desire for revenge against the men who have caused them pain, which could also be read as a reaction against colonialism itself. Yet the cautionary tale of the sundel bolong has two elements to it. On the surface, it cautions men against visiting sex workers in case it somehow causes

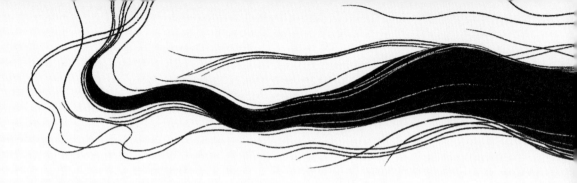

injury to the man, which could refer to disease as much as castration by a ghost. Dig a little deeper, and we see the tale also cautions men against treating a woman badly by getting her pregnant and avoiding responsibility.

Like many of her vengeful counterparts, the sundel bolong has made the transition into cinema, appearing in both *Sundelbolong* (1981) and *Legenda Sundel Bolong* (2007). Both films see the sundel bolong portrayed as a more sympathetic character, sexually assaulted but unable to obtain justice without resorting to ghostly power. This places her story into the "rape revenge" sub-genre of horror, in which her violence is wholly a reaction to the violence done to her. In the Marvel Animated anime version of *Blade* (2010–11), the sundel bolong appears as a type of vampire from Asia, which somewhat simplifies this nuanced figure. Yet the recasting of this angry spirit as a wronged woman denied justice in the Indonesian films gives us the best way to understand the sundel bolong: she's a woman ill-used by men, but she's not going to take her heinous treatment lying down.

Sundel Bolong **Indonesia**

CHAPTER 3

OBAMBO

Walking through a museum, a specific painting catches your eye. In it, a tiny hut stands beside a larger home, a length of white fabric hanging over its doorway. You've heard about them, but never seen one before; it can only be an obambo house.

The obambo is a spirit found in the lore of Central Africa. For some, it is entirely evil and could possess people or cause illness. For others, it is a ghost. For these latter groups, the obambo is a spirit of the dead who lives in the bush, often after not receiving the proper burial rites. The 19-century writer and journalist W. H. Davenport Adams described how the obambo might wish to settle near their family instead of wandering endlessly in the jungle. When this happened, the obambo approached a family member to ask them to build a house for the obambo near that of the family. The relative gathered the family that night, and the women of the family sang and danced for the obambo's benefit. They built a small house near the relative's home and hung a white cloth over the door. The next day, everyone gathered at the obambo's grave and made a small idol to represent the obambo. They put some of the earth from the grave on the bier they used to carry the body to the grave, and they put the bier and the grave dirt inside the newly built house. People continued to offer food to the obambo in exchange for their help.

In other parts of Central Africa, particularly for the Commi people, the obambo is believed to be a specific spirit, rather than a ghost. The spirit caused illness if it managed to possess a living person, taking up residence in their bowels, and no doctor could cure the patient until the obambo was driven out. Only making noise could accomplish this task; the more noise the better. Crowds surrounded the patient to beat drums, fire guns, sing and shout, or make as much noise as possible. The 19th-century French-American anthropologist Paul Du Chaillu noted that the patient often died before the obambo could be driven out.

It's worth keeping in mind where some of these stories come from, since they were often collected by white writers or anthropologists in Africa. Their preconceptions of the continent as a superstitious or uncivilized place shaped the bias with which they related what they saw or heard while spending time among local populations. While their attempts to describe rituals aimed to be objective, the racist language used in the commentary surrounding the description undermines whatever lore they wanted to capture. Their descriptions of illness also betray how little these white writers understood the symptoms of various conditions, such as epilepsy, which might explain the sickness and deaths of the people they observed who were possessed by an obambo.

ADZE

You lie back, listening to the high-pitched squeal of mosquitoes beyond the net hanging around your bed. They scream in frustration that they can't reach you. Footsteps knock against the floorboards, stopping outside your room, and you roll over in time to see a firefly squeeze through the gap beneath the door. It flies around, scattering the mosquitoes, as if searching for a hole in the net. It is just a firefly… isn't it?

The adze is a monster from the lore of the Ewe people in Ghana, Benin, Togo, and Nigeria. It takes the form of a firefly, mosquito, or beetle, entering the home through keyholes or cracks around doors or windows. Once inside, it will feast on human blood—though bloodsucking is only one of the side effects of an adze attack. They can also cause disease or damage an individual's standing in the community. In some regions, the adze favors female victims, while in others, they prefer the blood of children. If blood is scarce, the adze might consume coconut water or palm oil, but it depends on blood for vitality. You can't ward off the adze, which either drains their victim's life force or possesses them.

A possessed human is called an adzetos, and they can shapeshift at night. A ball of light might emerge from their nose or mouth, or the top of their head, and take the form of an insect or owl to travel large distances. In this form, the adzetos feeds on the life force of victims. Given the appearance of the adzetos as a ball of light, the firefly becomes a logical choice of insect to be associated with the adze. While the adze is most often depicted in firefly form, it also takes human form. If you force an adze into its human form, it will plead for its life and offer you anything to spare it. Sparing an adze's life will make it your ally.

It takes the form of a firefly, mosquito, or beetle, entering the home through keyholes or cracks around doors or windows.

Possession might also manifest as mental illness, a streak of bad luck, infertility, or addiction, among other things. Women are considered more open to possession

Adze   Togo, Benin, Ghana, and Nigeria

than men, and some believe witches were adzetos. Those who display jealousy towards others might be accused of adze possession, whether it is a woman jealous of her husband's other wives, or a poor person jealous of the wealth of a rich person. This assumption that women are more susceptible to adze possession mirrors wider narratives around women being more susceptible to evil forces, something we see in witchcraft accusations across the world.

The adze is most active at night in its bloodsucking form, seeking victims at their most vulnerable. Some sources describe them as an African vampire, and while similarities with vampires do exist, that also risks erasing cultural differences that make the adze specific to west Africa. After all, the effects of a possessed victim don't appear in wider vampire lore, while the adze's preference for children also highlights the vulnerability of this social group. The link between the adze and the vampire dates to 1906, when the German missionary Jakob Spieth recorded stories of the adze. He chose to interpret the adze using Western ideas, rather than investigate it within its own cultural setting. It's unsurprising that missionaries tried to link the adze with the Devil, which explains why praying at the victim, or carrying out an exorcism, became the method of choice to oust an adze from a possessed human.

The adze is most active at night in its bloodsucking form, seeking victims at their most vulnerable.

It's difficult to pinpoint where legends of the adze came from. The Ewe people arrived in the area that is now Togo and Ghana in the 13th century, but how the adze came into being varies across different legends. In one origin story, the first adze was a mortal witch. After working with dark powers in search of immortality, she ended

108

up becoming an adze: immortal, but needing to drink blood. Many historians suggest adze stories might have helped explain malaria or other diseases carried by insects. But as artist Adwoa Botchey points out, the adze and its links with jealousy in the community mean it also reflects concerns about preserving social harmony.

Surprisingly, the adze isn't seen as wholly bad. In some communities, the adze provides protection against external threats to the community. The locals might appease the adze with offerings of coconut water or palm oil in exchange for its protection. Helen Nde, curator of the Mythological Africans online platform, which explores African mythology and folklore, explains the adze can be understood as a spiritual power and force of creativity, both of which can be wielded for good or bad, depending on the individual. The monstrous adze is an example of this power as malevolent sorcery, and it is only within this context that we can understand the adze—so banish those vampiric notions altogether.

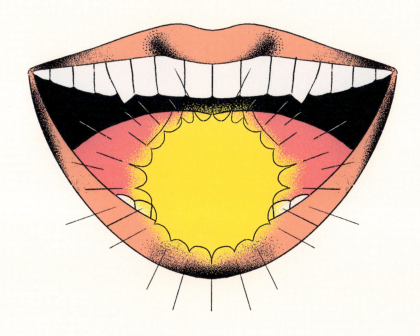

Adze

Togo, Benin, Ghana, and Nigeria

109

MADAM KOI KOI

Night fell hours ago, yet you lie in bed, listening to the gentle snores of your fellow students. You decide to go to the bathroom, but you pause as you cross the dormitory. A clicking in the corridor makes your blood run cold, and the dreaded "koi koi" noise sends you diving for cover beneath your sheets. The bathroom can wait; nothing could prise you out of bed while Madam Koi Koi prowls the corridors.

Madam Koi Koi is a popular Nigerian urban legend, as this vicious teacher haunts boarding schools at night, favoring hallways, dormitories, and toilets. Students in boarding schools are advised to stay in their rooms if they hear her coming. Those studying at day schools don't escape her wrath since she also haunts their toilets, appearing to students who arrive too early or leave too late. In some stories, she is never seen and only heard, while in others, she flings open doors, whistles, or even slaps students. She's often depicted wearing red high heels, and the "koi koi" sound of these heels in the hallway gives her such a distinctive name. Many schools have their own version of the legend—so widespread is the story that Netflix Nigeria made a two-part movie about it, *The Origin: Madam Koi Koi* (2023).

> **She's often depicted wearing red high heels, and the "koi koi" sound of these heels in the hallway gives her such a distinctive name.**

One origin story sees her cast as a fashionable teacher, famed for her shoes. But she was fired from the school for being physically abusive towards students, slapping a student so hard that she injured their ear. Madam Koi Koi swore she'd get her revenge, but died in an accident on her way from the school after being fired. The curse tied her to the world of the living, and students soon began hearing the sound of her heels in the hallways after lights out. In an alternative version of this story, Madam Koi Koi was a pleasant teacher, but only became vengeful after the students caused her to lose her job. The outcome is the same; she stalks the school hallways at night.

In another version from southern Nigeria, Madam Koi Koi sleeps in a grave at the school, originally made for a founding member of the school, only leaving the grave

Madam Koi Koi — Nigeria

to search for her missing red shoe. In this version, she will only stop haunting the school when she finds the shoe, but her coming and going from the grave is used to explain a crack in the gravestone.

A different version again casts her as a physically abusive teacher, except the violence she inflicted went unpunished as the school failed to investigate. The students decided to pay her back and seized her one evening as she was leaving. They gagged and beat her, while one student tore off one of her heels and attacked her with it. The students killed her, dumping her body beyond the school's fence to make it look like a random killing. One by one, the students involved disappeared in mysterious circumstances, until only the student who killed Madam Koi Koi with the shoe remained. Despite confessing to what they had done,  and telling everyone he heard high heels in his dormitory every night, no one took him seriously. Eventually, the student investigated the source of the sound and was found dead, beaten senseless, the next day. The school closed and the students were transferred elsewhere. But they told their new classmates what happened, and every time they did so, students began hearing the clicking of high heels at night. Any students who saw her disappeared—although it's unclear how anyone knew the student had seen her if they'd vanished.

…the students involved disappeared in mysterious circumstances, until only the student who killed Madam Koi Koi with the shoe remained.

Madam Koi Koi 💀 Nigeria

The transfer of Madam Koi Koi to new schools with each telling of her story is an interesting twist, allowing the ghost to go viral beyond any original event that inspired the legend, yet it also makes it difficult to pinpoint where the story originally began. This quality is what makes the Madam Koi Koi story more of an urban legend than folklore. You can spot urban legends most notably through a lack of names; in this case, Madam Koi Koi's real name is missing, as are the names of any students caught up in the events that explain what happened. There is no date attached to the events either, making it difficult to verify or link the story to real-life cases. It's possible that students invented the story to scare each other, as a form of children's folklore, in which students pass on stories between each other without any involvement of adults. They may have also encoded information about real teachers who resorted to violence within the legend as a warning to others. The version in which day school students are targeted if they arrive early or leave late is telling. Yet it's equally possible that teachers made up the legend to keep students in their rooms at night, using Madam Koi Koi as a deterrent to ensure compliance with school rules.

It's possible that students invented the story to scare each other, as a form of children's folklore...

OGBANJE

You sit in the park with your new friend; you only met her the night before, but you feel like you've known her for a lifetime. She looks up at the brilliant blue sky and announces it will rain. You laugh it off since the sky suggests otherwise, but she seems certain. It's her turn to laugh when dark clouds roll in 15 minutes later, dumping their contents over you both. How did she know?

The ogbanje is an Igbo spirit that reincarnates multiple times. While some sources refer to them as evil, their story is more nuanced than that. They belong in a liminal existence, present in the human world through birth but still tied to their ogbanje siblings in the spirit world, returning to their spirit family when they die. Yet their appearance in the world of the living causes pain and grief, since they often die suddenly, both before and after birth, though also as an older child. Some consider their role as bringing grief to the family into which they're born, like tricksters, though writers like Chinelo Eze note they have little say in how often or where they reincarnate. No one knows why they reincarnate so many times, especially within the same family, but it has led some to think the family is being punished for a secret wrong, or that an unpleasant ancestor is behind it. Families might suspect a child was an ogbanje if they had the same birthmarks or spoke the same first words as an earlier child who had died.

The ogbanje will bury a stone called an iyi-uwa somewhere secret; as long as these stones remain hidden, they can keep being born into the human world. A medicine man might be brought in to find the iyi-uwa; discovering the amulet breaks the connection with the spirit world so the ogbanje can live a normal life, otherwise, they might die suddenly to rejoin the spirit world or return to torment the family again.

Some think the ogbanje explains fertility issues, such as a string of miscarriages, sudden infant death syndrome, or health problems like sickle-cell anemia that appeared during childhood. Clinical psychiatrist Sunday T. C. Ilechukwu suggests the belief in ogbanje is a response to Nigeria's high infant mortality. Developments in medical science mean the stories of ogbanje are less common nowadays, yet writer Michael Chiedoziem Chukwudera points out that the ogbanje is about more than just sickness in children; they have a different relationship with the spirit world than normal humans, giving them abilities like foretelling the future. Contemporary novelist Akwaeke Emezi even identifies as an ogbanje, allowing for a new interpretation of the ogbanje identity as a form of empowerment and reminding us that there are different ways to view identity outside of those traditionally available within the West.

Ogbanje — Nigeria

SASABONSAM

Your friend sends you a video on social media, and you watch the shaky phone camera footage. The person with the phone wildly moves the frame through a forest, their panting loud through your speakers. Curiosity turns to horror when a large, dark shape drops out of the trees, lunging towards the camera. A wet thud and a soul-piercing scream fill the air before the camera drops to the ground and the video ends. "What did I just watch?" you type back. Your friend simply replies: "If only he hadn't gone into the forest on a Thursday".

The sasabonsam is a creature in the lore of the Akan people in Ghana, Togo, and Côte d'Ivoire. American anthropologist Joseph John Williams described the sasabonsam as large and hairy, with long legs, bloodshot eyes, and feet that pointed in both directions. Williams suggested the earliest versions of the sasabonsam may have been a misidentification of a gorilla. In other descriptions, it has a bearded face, horns, claws, and sharp teeth. It is depicted as skinny with prominent ribs, while its bat wings give it the power of silent flight. It is rumored to sit in high branches and dangle its legs to catch hunters, though it also sleeps in tree hollows. The sasabonsam is supposed to drink human blood, though it might also eat them.

Writer J. B. Danquah included a photograph of a sasabonsam carving, attributed to artist Osei Bonsu, in a newspaper article in 1939. The article quotes a youth who was part of the crowd watching the carving being photographed. He told the story of a man who killed a sasabonsam after he found it asleep in a tree hollow. He brought it to town to display the remains, which, the youth said, were strikingly similar to those in the carving. The main discrepancy between the sasabonsam and the carving was the length of the creature's arms; the carving's arms were too short.

Despite its monstrous appearance and tendency to feed on humans, the sasabonsam is also a forest protector. As research fellow Genevieve Nrenzah explains, the sasabonsam preys on those who venture into the forest on a Thursday, a day of rest for the Akan people, which gives the land an opportunity to replenish itself. It also explains the disappearances of hunters who went missing in the forest when they broke this rule.

It's possible the sasabonsam is a cautionary tale, designed to warn people about the dangers of going into the forest alone. Yet it also warns people to respect the forest and its laws. While the incoming Christians portrayed the sasabonsam as the Devil in the 20th century, emphasizing the evil in its terrifying actions, the best way to avoid the sasabonsam is to abide by forest laws.

POPOBAWA

You walk through the forest towards the campsite, where sleeping bags huddle around a crackling fire pit and your friends toast crumpets over the flames. While your group enjoys outdoor adventures, your local guide explains that in the past, people chose such sleeping arrangements to escape the clutches of malicious spirits. Something flutters overhead, throwing its shadow onto the path in front of you. You remark that the shadow looks like a bat and your guide mutters something you don't quite hear.

In early February 1995, people on Pemba Island in the Zanzibar Archipelago started to report nocturnal attacks by an evil spirit, the popobawa. "Popobawa" is its Swahili name, where *popo* is "bat" and *bawa* is "wing". The popobawa can shapeshift through different forms, though it casts a bat-like shadow at night. Stories of the malevolent creature echoed earlier reports of similar attacks that took place in 1964, following the Zanzibar Revolution.

> **The popobawa can shapeshift through different forms, though it casts a bat-like shadow at night.**

The shapeshifting popobawa attacked sleeping victims, and the reports are truly frightening. Victims recalled a disgusting smell, followed by sleep paralysis in which they were awake but unable to move. While the paralysis sounds similar to stories of Pantafica (p.48), other elements of the story are far worse; the popobawa sometimes adopted human form to suffocate or sexually abuse its victim. Strangely, the spirit threatened to return if the victim didn't report the experience, which may explain the sudden influx of reports, triggering widespread panic that spread to other islands.

People began sleeping in groups for safety, often outdoors in forests, or indoors in mosques. Some villages hired witch doctors to identify popobawa, and locals might be accused, suffering lengthy interrogations in search of confessions. Some victims of these attacks were badly beaten, despite their protestations of innocence.

Popobawa Zanzibar

Other villages managed to emerge unscathed; interestingly anthropologist Martin Walsh suggests that these villages were the ones that retained their indigenous rituals and practices, perhaps keeping the popobawa at bay because of this.

The panic on Pemba subsided after a couple of months, but it turned violent when it reached Zanzibar Town on the island of Unguja. In early April 1995, a group of frightened locals accused a stranger of being a popobawa, since he wore a charm around his neck—something believed to cause the awful smell that accompanies a popobawa visit. The group fell upon him with machetes and clubs, and beat the man to death. It later emerged that the stranger was due to be taken to a psychiatric hospital.

The following day, rumor spread that a body believed to be that of a popobawa was being held at a mortuary. It seemed the popobawa had turned up in the city, carrying a jar containing an unknown substance and a cow's tail. A witch doctor gave chase and seized the jar and cow's tail, at which point the popobawa transformed into a human. A mob formed who set upon the man, killing him. After his body was taken to the mortuary, crowds gathered to catch a glimpse of a dead popobawa. The deaths did little to quell public fear of the popobawa.

It seemed the popobawa had turned up in the city, carrying a jar containing an unknown substance and a cow's tail.

Both Zanzibar and Pemba had endured popobawa panics before, but the 1995 incident took off in a way that earlier ones hadn't. A range of individuals were blamed for the attacks, including foreigners and the mentally ill, with those accused publicly

120

attacked in an effort to end the panic. Since the well-known panic of 1995, there have been a handful of smaller panics, in 2000 and 2007.

Different stories have circulated to try to explain what happened. Some thought popobawa emerged from battles between sorcerers. Another version claimed a sheikh lost control of a jinn in the 1970s which led to the attacks, thereby linking tales of the popobawa with jinn belief. A possible political explanation also exists, since the first popobawa attacks began after the 1964 Zanzibar Revolution, while the 1995 attacks coincided with the first multi-party elections in the region. According to one theory, the ruling party might have deliberately spread panic to dissuade the population from voting for their rivals.

Walsh suggests that the violence of the region's colonial past also played a role in the panic, with the popobawa representing the fears of ordinary people during the height of enslavement. Combined with the stress of political tensions, the situation boiled over into panic, with violence directed at strangers, rather than each other. Writer Benjamin Radford points out that there is no single explanation for the popobawa. More than a demonic creature conjured during sleep paralysis, it also plays a role in culture and politics, straddling the divide between folklore, urban legend, and human experience—and we can only wait to see if it will return.

UNIONDALE HITCHHIKER

Miles of long, straight road unfold in front of your car, desert landscape stretching away from the tarmac on either side. Your gaze alights on something that stands out in such an unforgiving place: a woman standing at the side of the road. You pull up beside her and ask if she'd like a lift. After all, it'll take her hours to get wherever she's going on foot. She accepts and climbs into the back seat. As you drive on, you try to start a conversation, but her silence tells you she doesn't want to talk. That's fair, you think, she's trusting her life with a stranger. Except the next time you glance in the rearview mirror, the backseat is empty. You pull over and turn around, but she's gone. It's as if she was never in the car at all.

The Karoo is a swathe of semi-desert in South Africa, popular for its beautiful scenery and spectacular geology. Uniondale is a small town in the region, a town once known for building wagons and processing ostrich feathers. Now, it's more famous for its resident ghost, the Uniondale Hitchhiker.

On Good Friday in 1968, a young couple headed along the Barandas-Willowmore road, their Volkswagen Beetle lashed by heavy rain. Maria Roux slept in the backseat while her fiancé drove. In the early hours, when they were around 12 miles from Uniondale, Maria's fiancé lost control of the car, which overturned. Maria was killed.

Uniondale Hitchhiker

South Africa

> **In the early hours, when they were around 12 miles from Uniondale, Maria's fiancé lost control of the car, which overturned. Maria was killed.**

Eight years later, on Good Friday in 1976, a man spotted a woman hitchhiking along the same stretch of road. She told him her destination and they set off. After a short time, she vanished out of the car without warning, leaving the young driver understandably distressed. He reported it to police who followed him in their car to the spot where she vanished. One police officer later reported seeing the driver's passenger door open and close on its own.

Other drivers reported similar experiences after stopping to pick up a female hitchhiker from the lonely stretch of road, only to find that she'd vanished out of the car just a few miles into the journey. In some stories, drivers even saw the car door open and close, while others reported hearing her laugh, or felt a sudden chill in the car. Drivers reported that beyond providing a destination, their hitchhiker refused attempts at conversation. In some accounts, journalists showed photographs of Maria to these drivers, who identified her as being their mystery hitchhiker.

> **In some stories, drivers even saw the car door open and close, while others reported hearing her laugh, or felt a sudden chill in the car.**

Maria doesn't only stop drivers for a lift. Motorcyclists have even reported encounters, phantom arms suddenly encircling their waist as they pass the crash site. One motorcyclist was so terrified by the experience that he accelerated to try to lose the ghostly passenger. The ghost struck blows against his helmet, as if telling him to slow down, and only vanished at 44 mph. Another motorcyclist stopped to pick her up and handed her his spare helmet. When the bike twitched after a mile or so, the rider feared his passenger had fallen off, but when he turned to check

Uniondale Hitchhiker · South Africa

on her, there was nobody on the back of the bike. He retraced the route, fearful she might be lying in the road, but it was empty for miles in both directions. Even more terrifying, the spare helmet was exactly where he'd left it before he handed it to his passenger.

That the encounters always occur on Good Friday is notable. Like Fisher's Ghost (p.82), the Uniondale Hitchhiker offers us an example of a common type of ghost that appears in stories all over the world: the phantom hitchhiker, or vanishing hitchhiker. These stories include common ingredients, in which the hitchhiker is usually female and vanishes from inside a car while en route. In many versions of the legend, the driver reaches the address given by the hitchhiker, only to discover she died some years earlier. Sometimes, the hitchhiker leaves a physical item in the car, and the driver seeks to return it. The hitchhiker tends to appear on the anniversary of her death, though it's unclear why they disappear and do not complete the original journey.

Jan Harold Brunvand published his non-fiction book, *The Vanishing Hitchhiker*, in 1981, bringing the concept of these phantom hitchhikers to wider public awareness. Brunvand traced the concept back to the 1870s and found similar stories all over the world. In some areas, the phantom hitchhiker is actually a local deity, mixing with the community. Other alternatives include the hitchhiker making some kind of prophecy before they disappear. Where the 1986 thriller film *The Hitcher* showed the dangers of picking up hitchhikers who turn out to be murderous, the phantom hitchhiker perhaps acts as a caution against picking up strange passengers.

Uniondale Hitchhiker South Africa

125

AÏCHA KANDISHA

You walk along the empty street, your footsteps echoing against the darkened buildings. It's so quiet that you'd almost feel like the last person alive if it weren't for the cat crying in the distance. An empty lot yawns between apartment buildings, the shadows thick like syrup beyond the pavement. Movement catches your attention and you notice a figure standing in a large pool of stagnant water in the center of the lot. It stares at you, apparently inviting you closer and challenging you at the same time. You glance at the pool and see the figure's goat legs reflected on its surface. Shaking your head breaks the figure's hold and you hurry away down the street. You only stop running when you make it back to your hotel.

Aïcha Kandisha is a towering figure in Moroccan folklore, appearing as a beautiful but dangerous woman with dark hair that moves like smoke. In some versions of the story, she is a serpent from the waist down, while in others, she has the legs of a goat or a camel. Sources disagree as to her true nature; in some, she's described as one of the water jinn, while others see her as a separate spirit from the jinn. Yet the stories all agree on her stunning, almost indescribable beauty.

Her story is around five centuries old, although mystery obscures her origins. In some retellings, she was a human sorceress, turned into a demon by the lover who betrayed her. In other, less common versions, she died in childbirth and the experience turned her into a malevolent spirit bent on revenge, a little like the Sundel Bolong (p.98).

> **In some retellings, she was a human sorceress, turned into a demon by the lover that betrayed her.**

Some writers suggest Aïcha Kandisha derives from a real historical figure within the nomadic tribes of Morocco. When Portuguese troops attacked in the 15th century, the nomadic tribes resisted their attempts to colonize the country. A woman called Aïcha Kandisha carried out attacks against the Portuguese, who repeatedly failed to capture her. Her favorite technique involved luring soldiers away from their

Aïcha Kandisha Morocco

127

comrades with her beauty so resistance fighters could kill them. The Portuguese called her La Condessa, or the Countess, which is what her Moroccan nickname of Kandicha is based on. In some versions, she waited until the soldiers fell asleep and sneaked into their tents to slit their throats. The sheer number of deaths among the Portuguese troops led people to suspect there must be something supernatural about her.

While alone in the wilderness, she became a malevolent spirit, intent on punishing men, and it is this version that lingers in more contemporary tellings of her legend.

In some versions of the story, she continued to haunt the area after she died, attacking men who traveled alone at night. Her goats' legs (or just cloven feet in some retellings) gave away her identity, and recognizing her in time offered men the chance to escape. Those who failed to recognize her, or perhaps willingly overlooked the hooves in the face of such beauty, never returned home. In other versions of the legend, she swore revenge after the Portuguese slaughtered her family. While alone in the wilderness, she became a malevolent spirit, intent on punishing men, and it is this version that lingers in more contemporary tellings of her legend.

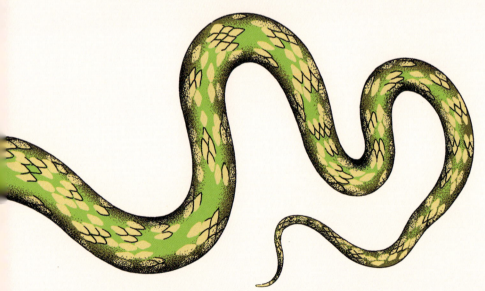

In contemporary stories, she is a fearsome jinn who targets lone men outside at night, although she also haunts bodies of water, empty streets, or abandoned spaces. After luring men in with her fabulous looks, she crushes them with her snake's body, eats their soul, or drinks their blood. The best defense is to avoid her, although some suggest the pure of heart have nothing to fear from her. Others think verses from the Qur'an help to ward her off. It's a shame that in most versions of the legend, Aïcha Kandisha's anti-colonial roots have often been obscured in the quest to portray her as a man-hating monster. The stories that acknowledge the historical figure behind the legend help to show how folklore and oral storytelling traditions become valuable tools to preserve and share information down the centuries.

Surprisingly, you can summon Aïcha Kandisha by pouring boiling water down the drain—although only those foolish enough to be in love with her would deliberately catch her attention in this way. As writer and researcher Asmae Ourkiya explains, if a man summons Aïcha Kandisha, she'll seduce him with her beautiful looks, and then show him her terrifying true face before possessing him.

Aïcha Kandisha remains a figure of fascination for storytellers, inspiring stage plays and films in recent years. While there is a tendency towards depicting her as a terrifying monster or dangerous jinn, her historical backstory makes her a more nuanced figure than she first appears. Is she a resistance fighter, avenging the deaths of her family and protecting her culture from an invading colonial force? Is she a water jinn with a taste for male flesh? Or is she both?

Still, if you find yourself in Morocco, you might want to avoid pouring boiling water down the drain or walking the streets alone at night...

CHAPTER 4

North America & Caribbean

JUMBEE

You sit on the back of your friend's scooter, clinging to him as he speeds towards what he calls Jumbee Corner. The evil demons of the island congregate here at night, ready to jump out at the unwary. As you hit the apex of the corner, his headlight goes out, throwing the road ahead into darkness. You squeal and he yells, "Jumbees!" The headlight flickers back into life and the road ahead remains empty, but your heart pounds all the way home. He assures you it was just a loose wire in the headlight. You hope he was right.

Jumbee is a catch-all term for a range of evil spirits in the Caribbean, which is sometimes spelled "jumbie" or "jumby". As an example, babies who died before baptism became the douen, mimicking adult voices to lure children into the woods. The churile is a female jumbee created when a mother dies in childbirth. She cries at night, looking for her baby. The lagahoo is a half-human, half-wolf male jumbee. Sometimes the lagahoo takes the form of a man covered in chains carrying a coffin.

Concepts of the jumbee vary between cultures, but a common point is that evil people remain evil after death, becoming the jumbee (although admittedly this doesn't quite fit the douen's origin story). Jumbees only come out after dark, and writer Judy Simmons explains that a sharp bend in a road on the island of Bequia was named "Jumbie Corner" since people believed jumbees gathered there at night. People avoided walking there alone after sunset.

In Guyana, one jumbee is the Ole Higue, the Guyanese version of the soucouyant. During the day, she lives among humans, taking the form of an introverted old lady. When night falls, she takes off her skin and streaks across the sky as a ball of fire. She picks out a victim and shrinks to fit through the keyhole. Once inside, she feeds on her victim's blood while they sleep. You can keep her out by leaving the key in the lock overnight or, if you can find her skin, covering it in hot peppers which will burn her when she tries to put it back on. Another way to protect yourself is to scatter rice across the entrance to your house, causing her to stop to count them all, like Pantafica (p.48).

There are plenty of other methods to avoid jumbees. Some jumbees like the douen either don't have feet, or have backward-facing feet. Leaving shoes outside your front door will distract them with trying on the shoes and they'll forget to enter your home. Like countless other spirits, jumbees can't cross running water, so crossing a river can take you out of harm's way. If you get home late at night, walk backwards through the door or spin in a circle before you open the door to stop the jumbee from following you inside.

DUPPY

A full moon hangs low in the sky, throwing shadows across the road. Despite the moonlight, you remember what your host said about avoiding duppies, and you skip from shadow to shadow. Even though the street looks empty, twigs snap in the darkness behind you and a dog barks from inside an empty yard. You keep your gaze firmly planted on the shadows ahead, and use them like stepping stones to your host's house. The dog stops barking and the twigs stop snapping as you reach the door, where a horseshoe hangs beneath the knocker, and a fine layer of sand coats the verandah. You're safe now... aren't you?

In Jamaican lore, everyone has two souls. When a person dies, the good soul goes to heaven, while their other soul is stuck in the coffin for three days. If the correct burial rites aren't followed, the shadow of the earthbound soul will leave the grave and become a duppy. When the shadow of the earthbound soul leaves the body, it might appear as smoke, a blue mist, or even a swarm of flies.

Some lore notes that a benevolent duppy might guard its family or watch over children, though duppies are more often referred to as malevolent beings. Some writers consider the duppy as a form of jumbee (p.132). The spirits also appear in the religious practice of Obeah, which combines the religions of enslaved people from West Africa and, in some regions, also draws on Indigenous Caribbean practices.

Duppies most commonly take on the form of the human in life, wearing clothes they were buried in and eating and drinking like people. Yet they can also come in different forms, including snakes, calves, or even three-legged fire-breathing horses. They can take the form of any animal except donkeys or lambs (the reason for these particular exceptions is unclear).

> **When the shadow of the earthbound soul leaves the body, it might appear as smoke, a blue mist, or even a swarm of flies.**

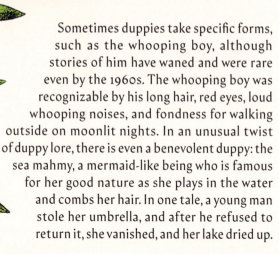

Sometimes duppies take specific forms, such as the whooping boy, although stories of him have waned and were rare even by the 1960s. The whooping boy was recognizable by his long hair, red eyes, loud whooping noises, and fondness for walking outside on moonlit nights. In an unusual twist of duppy lore, there is even a benevolent duppy: the sea mahmy, a mermaid-like being who is famous for her good nature as she plays in the water and combs her hair. In one tale, a young man stole her umbrella, and after he refused to return it, she vanished, and her lake dried up.

Duppies are believed to live in stands of bamboo or gather around kapok trees. They come out at night to harass their victims, when they might start fires or cause accidents around the home. Duppies can also wreak havoc in your life, causing your partner to leave you, or ensuring you lose your money. Some duppies even openly attack the living. Wives are especially vulnerable in the first nine days after their husband's death, since he might return as a duppy and expect sex from her—something that could induce infertility in her.

> **They come out at night to harass their victims, when they might start fires or cause accidents around the home.**

According to novelist Mack Little, there are four warning signs that a duppy might be nearby: smelling food when there's no obvious source, hearing a twig snap at night, having a spiderweb land on your face after dark, or hearing dogs bark when no dogs are nearby. Apparently, duppies are also recognizable by their feet, which whirl in a blur when they walk, hardly touching the ground.

As with many of the spirits in this volume, you can stop duppies from attacking you or your home by scattering sand or rice on the ground, forcing the duppy to stop to count it. If you cut 10 crosses into the ground with a knife, the duppy needs to circle the crosses 10 times, which gives you time to get away. If you're out at night, don't walk around in the moonlight where duppies can see you; stay in the shadows. Turning your clothes inside out is another option or, in a last resort, you can climb a tree if a duppy chases you.

Plant sweet basil by the door, or draw a circle on the door, to keep duppies out of your house. If a duppy has taken up residence in your home, then you can mix up cow dung, horn, and hoof, and burn the mixture to drive the duppy out. Carrying the shavings from the coffin of a person you feared might return as a duppy is also believed to protect you from that duppy.

It's unclear why you would want to seek a duppy out unless you were trying to avoid them, but if you want to see one, folklore advises you to look over your left shoulder. Another belief counsels you to collect water from a piebald horse's eye and put it in your own eye (perhaps best not to try this one at home).

While there are methods for warding them off, the best defense against duppies is to prevent them from rising from the grave in the first place. Some people recommend throwing parched peas into a grave during a burial or planting a shrub upside down over the grave to stop a duppy from returning. Laying a kapok tree limb on top of the coffin should also ensure the duppy stays out of the reach of the living. Let's hope they remain there.

Duppy 💀 Caribbean

HUPIA

Your island-hopping friends invite you to a sunset beach party, promising beautiful views of the Caribbean Sea. Music thumps from a Bluetooth speaker, people laugh over plastic cups of beer, and someone suggests a competition. How about telling ghost stories, they challenge. A local girl by the fire weaves a tale of faceless spirits seducing women and spiriting the living away into the darkness. You peer at your companions around the fire, checking that you can see their faces. After all, the sun has gone down, and hupias love nothing more than a good celebration...

The hupia is a spirit of the dead in Taíno culture, as opposed to the goeiza, or spirit of the living. The hupia can adopt many forms, including that of fruit, but it usually appears without a face or looks like a deceased loved one. If they choose the latter, they'll be almost indistinguishable from the living. After death, the dead are supposed to go to Coaybay, a place whose name has been variously translated as "dwelling place of the dead" or "abode of the absent ones". It is apparently remote and inaccessible to the living, viewed as a separate place with its own leader. The hupia leave Coaybay at night to move among the living. In the 15th century, Friar Ramón Pané recorded these Taíno beliefs about death and the afterlife, and while his accounts are the most contemporary writings about the Taíno culture from European first contact, his Catholicism also likely affected how he preserved the information.

The easiest way to spot a hupia is their lack of a navel or face. Their missing face signifies that they've lost their identity by passing into death (which also explains how they can adopt different forms, since they're no longer a unique individual). The missing navel shows that they lost their place in the Taíno community when they died. The navel is the original link to the mother, and in Taíno culture, determining your place in the community. Given the differences in belief about death between the Taíno and the European colonizers, it's difficult to tell if the ancient Taíno actually feared hupias or simply accepted them as part of life. In some legends, they seduced women or kidnapped anyone who was out after sundown. If a living man tried to embrace a hupia woman, she disappeared. In other legends, hupias slept during the day and ventured out at night to dance and celebrate. They were sometimes linked with bats, and were apparently fond of eating guava fruit.

The hupia made the leap to popular culture in 1990 in Michael Crichton's novel, *Jurassic Park*. In the book, the hupia became a vampiric creature that kidnapped small children at night. It's possible that this version of the hupia lives on in contemporary folklore, separated from the original hupia by both the passage of time and a change in belief system.

Hupia Caribbean

LA CIGUAPA

You head back along the trail toward the village where you're staying. At least, you think it's the right trail—now dusk has fallen, they all look the same. Suddenly, the forest falls silent. No more chittering of insects, or rustling in the undergrowth. Even the trees seem to be holding their breath. A moment later, a strange chirruping fills the air, and it sets all the hairs on your arms standing on end. You don't wait to see what's creating the sound—you simply run.

Such a sound could certainly be made by La Ciguapa, a creature in the folklore of the Dominican Republic. She's usually noted for her beauty, with a glorious mane of hair, hypnotic eyes, and a statuesque figure. In some accounts, she has dark brown skin, while in others, her skin is blue. Some legends tell of her hair being so long it wraps around her body like a dress, while others note she's only three feet tall.

The nocturnal La Ciguapa lives in the Dominican Republic's forests and mountains, only venturing into villages to look for food. In some stories, she sneaks into kitchens on her quest for dinner. In others, she lies in wait for lone men roaming outdoors at night, especially in the woods. She catches their attention with a series of chirp-like calls before luring them in with her hypnotic gaze. Men are often so entranced by La Ciguapa's beauty that they don't notice her backwards-facing feet (much like the jumbee, p.132), which give her away as being non-human. She either eats the men alive or captures their souls, depending on the story; some tales suggest she takes them back to her lair for sex before killing them. She's most likely to venture out on the night before the full moon. It's best to avoid La Ciguapa at all costs. You can tell if La Ciguapa is in the area if you're in a forest and all the usual woodland sounds fall silent. Avoiding eye contact with her stops her from bewitching you. Staying at home at night will also keep you safe, as she only targets those wandering outdoors.

La Ciguapa has similarities to European mermaids and the churel of India. Mermaids are believed to lure lone men to their deaths, although other figures around the Caribbean such as La Diablesse do likewise, making them a cautionary tale against following lusty appetites. Meanwhile, the churel and some types of jinn are also recognized by their backward-facing feet. These unusual feet also make it difficult to track La Ciguapa since it's not clear in which direction she's heading.

It's difficult to pinpoint the origins of the La Ciguapa legend, especially since so many variations exist, though she first appeared in print in an 1866 short story. That said, there are some who still believe La Ciguapa exists, haunting the forests and mountains. It's probably best not to venture into the woods at night, just in case.

La Ciguapa · Dominican Republic

DUNGARVON WHOOPER

The trail leads through a dense patch of trees, crossing tiny streams that feed the mighty Dungarvon River. You and your friends pick your way through the ferns towards the campsite, hoping to reach it before nightfall. As it is, sunset fast approaches and the lengthening shadows make it difficult to see where to put your feet. Suddenly, an unearthly scream splits the dusk, tearing through the trees like a whirlwind. You all freeze, torn between trying to work out what it is and where it is. It dies away so you hurry on, but it sets a pattern that follows you to the campsite. Scream, stop, scream, stop, on and on until night has truly fallen.

The Dungarvon Whooper (pronounced "hooper") tells the tale of a ghost that is heard, rather than seen, in the forests of New Brunswick. It prowls the Miramichi area, not far from the lands patrolled by the Headless Nun (p.146). In the early 19th century, lumberjack camps thronged these forests and a young Irish cook named Ryan found work in a camp near the Dungarvon River.

Described as handsome, tall, and strong, Ryan was well-liked by the men. He was famed for his loud holler, a quality prized among woodsmen, and a well-stuffed money belt. No one knew how he'd come by such an amount of cash, but given his popularity, no one asked.

> **The Dungarvon Whooper (pronounced "hooper") tells the tale of a ghost that is heard, rather than seen, in the forests of New Brunswick.**

Every morning, he made breakfast and prepared lunch for everyone, before hollering to wake everyone up. Usually, the woodsmen headed off to work, while Ryan remained at the camp alone. Yet one morning, the camp boss stayed at the camp with Ryan. Though respected and obeyed by the lumberjacks, this boss was a stranger to the area. When the men returned that afternoon, they found Ryan dead on the floor, and his money belt missing.

The camp boss claimed Ryan suddenly fell ill and died on the spot, but considering the strange circumstances and the missing belt, the woodsmen saw this for what it was: a likely story to cover a murder by the boss. A storm blew in, trapping the men in the camp, so they buried Ryan in the forest. On their way back to the camp, a frenzied series of screams and whoops tore through the howling gale. The screaming continued night and day until the woodsmen left in fear. They never returned.

On their way back to the camp, a frenzied series of screams and whoops tore through the howling gale.

In another version of the legend, it is Ryan—this time an Irish lumberjack—who is the murderer. While on a hunting trip, Ryan shot the camp cook, stole his money, and returned to camp. He claimed a bear had attacked them, knocking him out and dragging the cook into the forest. The lumberjacks headed into the woods to search

Dungarvon Whooper

Canada

for the cook, and Ryan made his escape while they were gone. The lumberjacks first heard the whooping and screaming while searching for the cook.

In both versions of the story, people continued to hear the whooping for years in the woods until a priest came in to lay the ghost to rest. He read passages from the Bible and made the sign of the cross. While some insist the priest was successful, others say you can still hear the Dungarvon Whooper even now, especially at sunset. Some people even report smelling frying bacon in the forest, insisting the cook's ghost is trying to tempt his murderer further into the woods.

An alternative explanation for the screaming claims that a train was lost in 1825 during the Great Miramichi Fire. The train plunged into the flames, never to be seen again, and some think the Whooper's screams are those made by the lost steam engine. Others insist locals dubbed the nightly train the Dungarvon Whooper, since the screech of its whistle resembled the phantom whoops and hollers in the woods. This explanation debunks the ghost story, providing a logical reason for the sound continuing in the area.

The earliest written version of the story comes from a Michael Whelan poem written in the early twentieth century. The story is notable for its reliance on sound, rather than the sight of the ghost. Though it may have a realistic explanation, with the scream of the train whistle confused with the scream of a ghost, it also relies on a similar tropes of a ghost seeking justice as in Fisher's Ghost (p.82) or the Greenbrier Ghost (p.152). The lumberjacks already had Ryan's body, so the ghost didn't need to show them where his remains were, but the ghost's screams in the woods alerted the lumberjacks to the fact he'd been murdered. Justice was never done because the murderer fled the scene of the crime, so the screams continued as a reminder of the crime that went unpunished. Perhaps the screams still tear through the woods, whether there's anyone to hear them or not.

Dungarvon Whooper — Canada

145

HEADLESS NUN

You follow the group of actors up the trail, taking your place with the rest of the audience when they strike up their next few lines of dialogue. They re-enact the foul murder of an 18th-century nun in the woods where it apparently happened. Chills run along your arms and you wish you'd worn another layer or two. Someone whispers your name behind you and you turn, expecting to see one of your friends. Instead, a figure in a long, dark cloak stands in the shadows cast by the trees. You can't work out how they whispered your name since it hits you with a jolt that they have no head.

The Headless Nun ghost of French Fort Cove, New Brunswick, is that of Sister Marie Inconnue, a French nun who lived in the area in the 18th century. This area was once home to a stone quarry and a sawmill, and the cove lies between Miramichi and Newcastle. In the 17th century, French settlers began building homes in Acadie, Nova Scotia. They became known as the Acadians, and the British forced them out of their homes, so the Acadians instead established the fort near the cove (hence the name, French Fort Cove). Sister Marie was in the area to assist the Acadians, having been sent to the region from France.

The nun's legend involves a gruesome murder taking place in 1758.

The nun's legend involves a gruesome murder that took place in 1758. As the story goes, Sister Marie left her home to either assist a difficult childbirth or to help an ill person. She was returning home late at night when she was attacked at the cove, some say by a trapper, others say by someone who was looking for treasure.

Why would a nun know where to find treasure? According to legend, the Acadians buried their valuables to keep them safe when they fled, telling Sister Marie where they were in case anything should happen to them. In this version of the story, sailors knew of Sister Marie's specialist knowledge and targeted the nun, trying to force her to divulge the location of the treasure. In another version of the story, Sister Marie ran a fund to help Acadian families in need, and she buried the money herself for safety reasons.

Whether she was attacked by a trapper or treasure-hungry sailors, Sister Marie was found dead the next day at the cove. She'd been decapitated, and no one ever found her head. Her headless ghost now haunts the cove, though it's difficult to tell whether she's guarding the treasure she died to protect, or if she's looking for her missing head. The Acadians returned Sister Marie's body to France, but it seems she can't rest without her head.

Her headless ghost now haunts the cove, though it's difficult to tell if she's guarding the treasure she died to protect, or if she's looking for her missing head.

Local author Doug Underhill researched the story and believes there is enough evidence to say the nun was murdered in the area. As for her restless spirit? Locals have encountered her ghost, including one man who reported she touched him on the back of his head. Shortly after, his hair turned white in three patches where she touched him. Other visitors report meeting the headless ghost who asks for their help, while others encounter the ghost carrying her own head, and asking for their help in burying the head with the body.

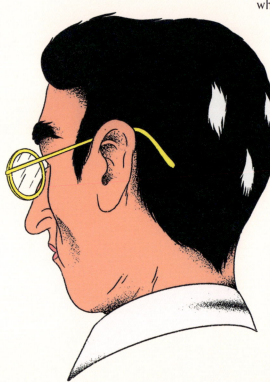

Stories of phantom nuns are common in the United Kingdom, though they're either associated with religious houses lost during the Dissolution of the Monasteries, or it is believed that the nuns were walled up alive after becoming pregnant with an illegitimate child. Yet in this tale from Canada, the nun avoids both the religious complexity of the Reformation and the scandal associated with illicit trysts. The emphasis remains on her

Headless Nun

Canada

148

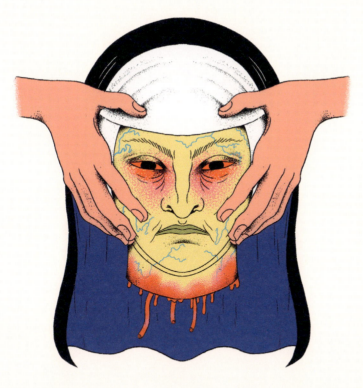

religious calling, her devotion to those she helped, and her apparent refusal to give in to the demands of her attackers. While a headless body would usually frustrate attempts at identification, the locals clearly knew Sister Marie well enough to identify her remains, suggesting her importance to the wider community.

The Headless Nun is typical of the type of ghost that actively seeks aid from the living, although it is not always obvious what form the aid should take.

The Headless Nun is typical of the type of ghost that actively seeks aid from the living, although it is not always obvious what form the aid should take. Unlike the phantom hitchhiker (p.122) who re-enacts their traumatic death every year, or the Greenbrier Ghost (p.152) who sought to unmask her killer, this type of ghost wants help to lay their remains to rest. In this way, the story continues the tradition begun with Athenodorous and the phantom man in chains in his Athens house (p.18). Hopefully, one day, someone can help Sister Marie find her way home.

RIDGEWAY GHOST

Your friend drives along the lonely stretch of road, pointing out snippets of the town's history as you chat. Suddenly, a sheep appears in front of the car, though it wasn't there a moment ago. Your friend swerves to avoid the animal, and when you turn in your seat to look back, the road is again empty. You glance into the fields lining the road, but none of them contain sheep. A pig loiters in one field, while a shadowy man cracks a whip in another. "I think we just saw the Ridgeway Ghost," says your friend, before crossing herself and speeding up.

Ridgeway, Wisconsin, is famous for having a ghost painted on the town water tower, and the figure looms large in the town's history. Welsh, Irish, Germans, and Norwegians settled in Ridgeway in the early 19th century, drawn by the prospect of work in the lead mines. The supernatural sightings began as early as the 1840s, with stories passed on by word of mouth.

The ghost primarily haunts Route 151 between Blue Mounds and Dodgeville, once described as the Old Military Road. While the earliest stories describe a dark, gigantic figure, the ghost takes different forms, including a dog, a sheep, a man with a whip, both young and old women, a pig, a horse, a headless horseman, and even a ball of fire. It appears out of nowhere, attacks someone, then vanishes. In past sightings, the ghost has ridden in carriages and murdered travelers. Yet it has also interacted with animals by scaring horses or milking cows dry.

A 1902 *New York Times* article tells the tale of Dr. Cutler of Dodgeville, who saw the ghost on three separate occasions, with the third encounter scaring him to death. The same article describes the experiences of John Lewis, who met a giant figure as he headed home, which picked him up and threw him around in the air. He attacked it with his knife and was found drifting in and out of consciousness the next day, though he died a few hours later.

No one can agree on the origin of the ghost. Some point to the murder of two teenage brothers at the saloon in 1840 as the starting point, while others claim it can be traced back to the murder of a man in a bar brawl during the 1840s. Horror writer J. A. Hernandez notes there is even a possibility that locals invented the stories in the 1850s to scare away any would-be troublemakers. Yet the ghost also shares similarities with the barguest (p.28) through its ability to adopt so many different forms. It's unclear how witnesses know they've encountered the Ridgeway Ghost, and not just an ordinary sheep or dog. This difficulty to pinpoint an origin, or even a definite form, shows the flexibility of many supernatural creatures.

GREENBRIER GHOST

You pause outside the courthouse and read about its history on the information board. An older woman in clothes too out of date to be vintage stops beside you. "That's where they had the trial, you know, for Trout Shue. He killed his third wife, and some say, he also killed the first two," she says. She nods and wanders away before you can reply. You look back at the building, and a shadowy figure peers out of an upstairs window. It might be a trick of the fading light, but you could swear the figure's head did a full 360° twist before it vanished.

For this ghost story, we need to look at the life of the woman who would become the ghost first. Zona Heaster was a young woman in love with a handsome blacksmith with a checkered past, Erasmus Stribbling Trout Shue. Yet her mother, Mary Heaster, counseled Zona not to marry him. No one knows if Mary knew about Shue's criminal record or previous two marriages. He abandoned his first wife, so she divorced him. Rumors abounded that he "accidentally" killed his 16-year-old second wife by dropping a brick on her head while fixing a chimney—though there is no proof that's what happened.

> **For this ghost story, we need to look at the life of the woman who would become the ghost first.**

What did Zona do? She ignored her mother and married Shue, some ten years older than her, in November 1896. According to the legend, Zona got married wearing the dress Shue later chose for her to be buried in. As the story goes, all seemed well between the pair, until one morning in January 1897. Shue went to a neighbor on the way to his forge, asking the family's son Anderson to check if Zona needed any help. She'd been unwell and Shue didn't want her out in the cold. When Anderson went looking for Zona, he found her dead at the foot of the stairs. By the time Dr. Knapp arrived, Shue had dressed Zona, putting a high collar around her neck. Dr. Knapp couldn't revive her and Shue insisted that no one else touch the body.

Following the burial, Mary Heaster came forward and accused Shue of murder. Her source was Zona herself, who'd appeared to her mother on successive nights to tell the story of her death. According to the story, Zona hadn't cooked meat as part of the supper, and Shue lost his temper. He'd snapped her neck, and Mary even claimed the ghost of Zona turned her head around on her neck to demonstrate how broken it was.

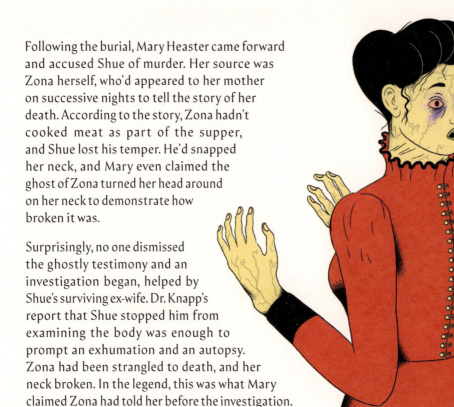

Surprisingly, no one dismissed the ghostly testimony and an investigation began, helped by Shue's surviving ex-wife. Dr. Knapp's report that Shue stopped him from examining the body was enough to prompt an exhumation and an autopsy. Zona had been strangled to death, and her neck broken. In the legend, this was what Mary claimed Zona had told her before the investigation. Witnesses later remembered the way the head of Zona's corpse dropped when unsupported on the way to the graveyard.

It's difficult to know what details were presented since the trial records were lost in a fire. Still, the jury returned the murder verdict in an hour, and Shue received a sentence of life imprisonment—although he died of flu three years later.

In 1910, someone interviewed Anderson about what he saw. He claimed to have followed a trail of blood into the house, and he found Zona dead on the dining room floor—not at the foot of the stairs. Writer Todd Atteberry suggests that Zona suffered a miscarriage, which explains why the doctor listed "childbirth" as the cause of death. Perhaps Shue attacked Zona out of anger when he realized Zona was losing his child.

A highway marker gives a short account of the tale, and its final words explain the importance of the story: "Only known case in which testimony from ghost helped convict a murderer". No one knows why Shue killed Zona, if indeed he did. Some point to his quick temper and behavior towards previous wives, labeling the murder as an unplanned outburst that went fatally wrong. Some of his relatives insisted he didn't kill Zona. The only evidence was her broken neck and Mary's testimony. No one produced Zona's ghost at the trial, but they didn't have to. People believed that a murdered daughter's ghost would appear to her mother, and Shue was already guilty in the court of public opinion.

Despite the fact that she never appeared again, Zona's ghost took on more importance than the facts of the case as the folk tale spread, and people often reference the story rather than the original events that inspired the tale. As we see from the tale of Fisher's Ghost (p.82), the ghost demanding justice appears in stories all over the world. Fisher's ghost wanted his remains to be found, while Zona's ghost wanted the truth to be known. Whether it was the truth is almost irrelevant to the story. One thing remains a crucial factor though—if Zona's ghost didn't appear to her mother, then how did Mary know of Zona's broken neck when even the doctor was unaware of it before the autopsy?

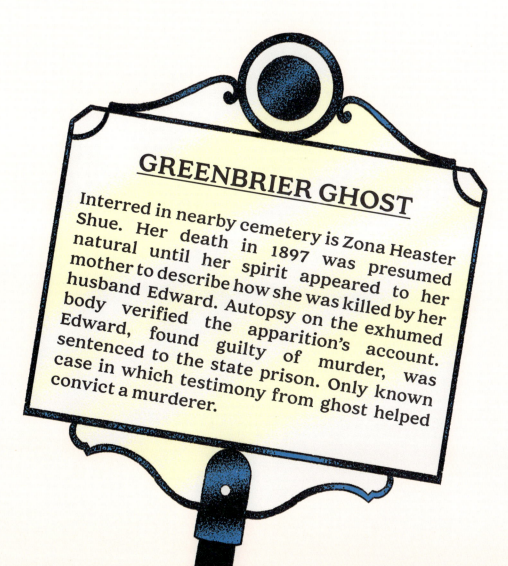

GREENBRIER GHOST

Interred in nearby cemetery is Zona Heaster Shue. Her death in 1897 was presumed natural until her spirit appeared to her mother to describe how she was killed by her husband Edward. Autopsy on the exhumed body verified the apparition's account. Edward, found guilty of murder, was sentenced to the state prison. Only known case in which testimony from ghost helped convict a murderer.

Greenbrier Ghost USA

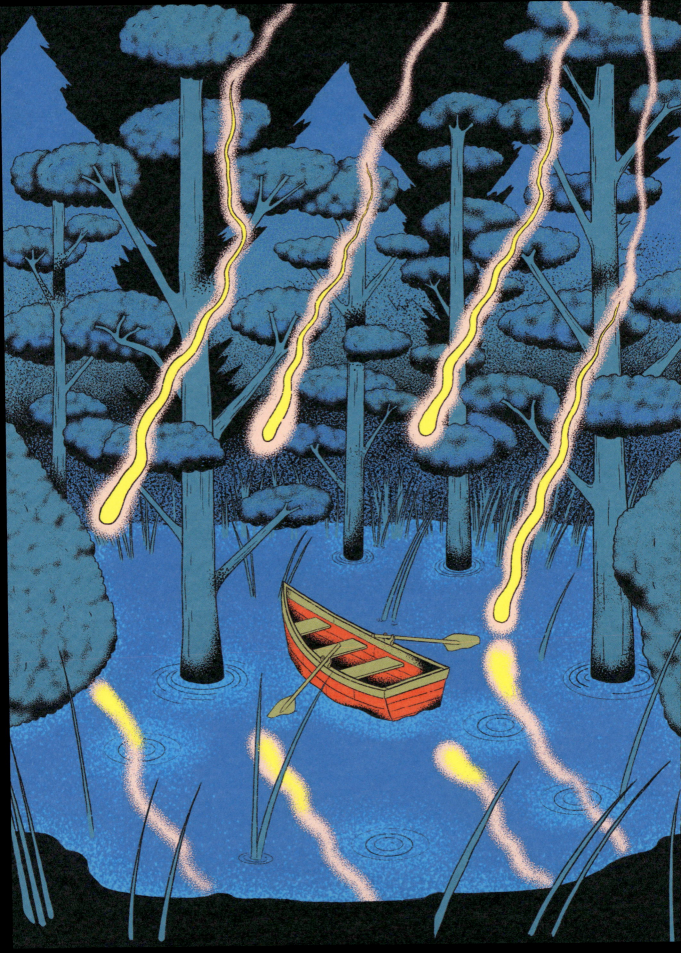

FEU FOLLET

The boat glides through the dark water, reflecting the night sky. Animals lurk in the shadows on the riverbank and insects flutter around the lanterns. You gaze into the darkness, your attention drawn to tiny lights flickering ahead. Their dancing is hypnotic and you want to get closer to see what they're doing. If only you could get closer... Suddenly, one of your companions pulls you back into the boat. "Don't look at them," he says. You look away, and the urge to clamber out of the boat wears off.

People translate "feu follet" as "marsh fire" or "crazy fire", depending on the source, although they're also referred to as "swamp fairies". Similar to the will-o'-the-wisp in European folklore, these balls of light the size of candle flames dance above the Louisiana bayou. It's unclear whether the lights are the fairy-like creatures themselves, like supernatural fireflies, or whether the lights are torches carried by tiny figures. For some, the feu follet is the spirit of the dead paying a last farewell. That loved ones would visit one final time is a comforting thought, and it could explain why some feu follet dance around cemeteries; the Bilbo Cemetery in Lake Charles, Louisiana has reported feu follet sightings since the 1840s.

Yet others think they are malevolent, deliberately drawing people into the swamp, either to drown them or get them lost. In this way, they are a cautionary tale; parents tell children stories of the feu follet to get them to avoid the swamp at night. Elsewhere, people think the feu follet is the spirit of a baby. They sometimes sneak into nurseries to steal baby breath at night. Some even think the feu follet are the spirits of pirates, bound to guard buried treasure forever. The lights will nearly always dance away from you, which is how they lead the unsuspecting—or treasure hunters—into the marsh. Not following them is an easy way to avoid a watery fate. Yet in one tale in Gonzales, Louisiana, a group of friends reported seeing a group of multi-colored lights in a field that appeared to head straight for them. Unsurprisingly, the friends scattered.

If you feel a feu follet is near, put iron on the ground between you and the spirit. They can't cross iron—another feature they share with European fairy beings. You can also scatter seeds behind you which forces the feu follet to count them, something common to many spirits in this book.

Science suggests these lights are caused by flammable methane. Decaying plant or animal matter creates the gas, which catches fire, and while this can be proven in the lab, it's difficult to test the theory out in the field. Any—or all—of the explanations could be true, so it's best to ignore any lights that dance in the darkness.

CHAPTER 5

Central & South America

HOMEM DO SACO

You wait at the bus stop—the road remains stubbornly empty. No, not quite empty. A lone figure strides up the pavement towards you, an older man wearing faded clothes and battered work boots. He snarls at you as he stalks by, revealing yellow teeth, and you shrink back to let him pass. He carries a burlap sack on his back, and as you watch him stomp away up the street, you could almost swear that the sack is wriggling.

The Homem do Saco, or Sack Man, roams the streets of Brazil, searching for naughty children. When he finds them, he grabs them and throws them in the sack he carries on his back—they're never seen again. He's often portrayed as a tall drifter or unhoused adult, and his impressive height intimidates those who encounter him. Beliefs around what he does with the children that he collects vary across the legend. In some versions of the story, he eats them, while in others he sells them, and in yet other stories, he turns the children into buttons or soap. The latter option aligns him with the dreaded pishtaco of Peru and Bolivia (p.174).

The Homem do Saco exists halfway between folklore and urban legend, since it's difficult to find reports of actual encounters with him. No one knows anyone seized by him, and while people attest to seeing many of the figures in this volume, the Homem do Saco seems far more elusive. Yet he also stalks the streets in Portugal and Spain, and those who recall being told stories of him remember being threatened that he would appear—but not warned of what he would do when he did. Folklorist Colin Horgan suggests such figures have historically been important because they make the concept of punishment seem tangible for young children, who might not otherwise understand more abstract notions around right and wrong.

Some think the legend only dates to the 1970s, perhaps based on older stories, although the appearance of such a figure in folklore around the world suggests he is an ancient bogeyman. He even appears in a surprising number of variations. In Iceland, this figure is the troll Grýla, who collects misbehaving children in her sack to add to her cooking pot. The babay lurks beneath beds in Russia, Belarus, and Ukraine to seize children who sneak out of bed, while El Roba Chicos snatches children in Honduras lore. There are strange crossovers between the Sack Man and Father Christmas in Europe and the Caribbean, although the more menacing Brazilian version appears all year round. The stories even reflect the more recent clown panics of the 1980s and again in 2016, in which people feared their children being stolen by nefarious clowns. The sheer number of variations suggests an urge to personify punishment for children—which is a far more comforting thought than the idea these bogeymen might be real.

Homem do Saco · Brazil

LA PLANCHADA

You lie in the hospital bed, your face turned towards the faint breeze sneaking in through the open window. The sounds of night-time traffic drift by, a welcome reminder that life continues even while you're recovering here. At least you'll be out soon, unlike the guy near the window. He seems at death's door, so you're glad when the nurse arrives for him. Her uniform looks dated compared to the other nurses, and she makes no sound when she moves. She chats to him in a low voice, and he soon falls asleep. You must doze off too, because the next thing you know, sunlight floods the room. The guy opposite sits up in bed, the very picture of health, telling the doctor about the nurse who visited last night. Your blood runs cold when the doctor tells him no nurse of that description works here.

It's easy to think of ghosts as the specters of long-dead figures from earlier centuries, yet the legend of La Planchada takes us to the 1920s and 1930s. It mostly appears at the Hospital Juarez in Mexico City, although the story has since spread to other hospitals. According to the legend, a phantom nurse roams the hospital, sitting for hours with the sickest patients in the depths of the night. When the stories first emerged in the 1930s, the patients described the nurse as wearing a uniform from the previous decade, but no one could explain what she'd done to heal them. All they knew was that they felt terrible before speaking to her, and they woke up having miraculously recovered during sleep.

La Planchada

Mexico

> ## According to the legend, a phantom nurse roams the hospital, sitting for hours with the sickest patients in the depths of the night.

Some witnesses have reported seeing her and thinking she was a real person, until noticing her shoes made no sound. Others have reported a faint blue glow around her, and feeling a sensation of calm when she's around. No one knows exactly who she is, although, in one origin story, she was a nurse who accidentally killed a patient. After death, she returned to save as many patients as she could to repay this

163

debt. A variation on this story sees her carry out a mercy killing for a terminally ill patient to end their pain. Another legend sees her as an actual angel, attempting to help humanity in the guise of a nurse.

Yet one story provides more detail than the others and names her as Eulalia. By all accounts, Eulalia was professional, dedicated, and compassionate, respected by patients and colleagues alike. Yet Eulalia was still human, and she began a romance with one of the hospital doctors. For the first few weeks, the love affair was passionate and Eulalia walked on air.

It was not to last, and the doctor's eye began to wander. He withdrew from Eulalia, preferring the company of younger nurses. While he never explained his change of heart, Eulalia couldn't help but notice his cold and dismissive demeanor, and she knew what that meant for their affair—it was over.

> **She never woke up again, with some whispering that she'd died of heartbreak in the night. Others suggested more sinister forces at play.**

One night, Eulalia went home after a difficult shift and lay on her bed to rest. She never woke up again, with some whispering that she'd died of heartbreak in the night. Others suggested more sinister forces at play.

In an alternative version of this legend, the doctor was secretly engaged to someone else. He left town, apparently to attend a conference, although a colleague revealed the doctor was actually on his honeymoon. Eulalia died shortly after, again apparently of heartbreak. However her death happened, Eulalia didn't rest for eternity. Patients and staff reported seeing a nurse patrolling the hospital corridors at night. She always wore a perfectly ironed uniform, which gave rise to her name of La Planchada, or "The Ironed Lady", and many believed it to be Eulalia, still hard at work.

Other spirits in this volume have ranged from the terrifying to the malevolent, or they have sought revenge or justice for their untimely ends. La Planchada is none of these things and instead is more like Philibert Aspairt in the Paris Catacombs (p.26). A benevolent spirit, La Planchada is believed to offer care throughout the night to the sickest patients, who often recover by morning. She continues to provide comfort where she can, and healing where it's needed most. This places her in a rare category of helpful or protective ghosts, who may still be eerie in nature, but offer no harm to those who encounter them. Whether these types of ghosts are driven by dedication to their job, or they haven't entirely accepted the fact that they've died, remains unknown.

A benevolent spirit, La Planchada is believed to offer care throughout the night to the sickest patients, who often recover by morning.

That said, staff leave her alone to do her job. She's a source of care for the patients but no one knows how she might react if challenged by a member of staff. We can only guess how she might respond if a doctor confronted her, especially one that might remind her of the doctor who broke her heart. So La Planchada continues her noble work in peace—and long may she do so.

La Planchada 💀 Mexico

165

LA PASCUALITA

There is a crowd of people by the store window. They disperse, revealing a mannequin clad in a flowing white bridal dress and veil. She looks far more realistic than most mannequins, her brown eyes seeming to track your approach. You stare at the veins on her hands and look up into her face. She has a soft, almost beatific smile, like a modern day saint's statue. And then she blinks.

The La Popular bridal store in Chihuahua, Mexico, has been open since the 1930s. It is most famous for the beautiful mannequin in the window, which always wears the latest bridal clothes. Yet, if you believe the stories, it's not actually a mannequin—it's the embalmed body of a young woman. According to the legend, the store's first owner, Pascuala Esparza, had a beautiful daughter. Tragically, she died on her wedding day (from either a black widow spider bite or a scorpion sting, depending on the story). When a beautiful new mannequin appeared in La Popular's window in March 1930, locals were suspicious. The skin looked too much like skin, the eyes too much like human eyes—it had to be a preserved human, rather than a mannequin. Worse, it bore an uncanny resemblance to Pascuala's own daughter, so the mannequin was dubbed "La Pascualita". The hands were particularly creepy, with their veins, wrinkles, and imperfect nails. Shop workers have revealed that the mannequin's legs even feature varicose veins. Mannequins rarely display that level of detail.

Shop assistants claimed they'd heard fabric rustle, or that the new mannequin moved when they weren't looking. If the mannequin didn't move, then her eyes certainly followed customers' movements around the store. Locals even said she came to life at night, and people stared at her after dark, waiting to see if she'd blink. The various owners since then have maintained that La Pascualita is just a mannequin, yet people remain convinced she is the embalmed daughter, animated by the lost bride's spirit. Another version of the story sees the mannequin animated by Pascuala Esparza herself since the strange events only began in 1967 when Pascuala died.

It feels like an urban legend, especially since some details have stuck, but not La Pascualita's real name. Local police once examined the mannequin and reported it was made of wax and plastic. Experts have pointed out that even an embalmed corpse would need to be stored in specific conditions to prevent deterioration—something that is unlikely in a shop window in Mexico. It would also need ongoing work to maintain the embalming since La Pascualita is handled regularly to change her dress. Yet there is something unnerving about such a realistic mannequin. Was she ordered from a specialist creator in Paris, as some versions of the legend suggest? Or is there truly a spirit lurking in the figure, moving its limbs and eyes to unnerve customers?

EL SILBÓN

You meander along the trail through the forest and your guide tells you about the area's history. Suddenly, a strange sound drifts towards you on the breeze. It's a mournful tune you don't recognize and the blood drains from your guide's face. He leads you to a rock pile where you hide in the shadows. You only creep out when the whistling gets louder, and he ignores your confused questions until the whistling dies away completely.

We find the legend of El Silbón, or The Whistler, in Los Llanos, a tropical grassland region east of the Andes. In one origin story, El Silbón's parents spoiled him by doing everything he demanded. One day, he instructed his father to bring deer home for dinner. When his father couldn't find one, El Silbón killed him, removing his liver and heart. He gave them to his mother to cook, and when his mother learned the truth about where they came from, she cursed El Silbón for eternity. In another origin story, his father caught him with a sex worker and killed her, so El Silbón killed him in retaliation. In yet another version, El Silbón's father accused his wife of infidelity, and their argument ended with his wife's death. El Silbón killed his violent father in a fit of fury. Whatever the version, what happened next remains the same. His grandfather punished El Silbón for patricide by lashing the boy's back to shreds. Next, his grandfather forced him to carry a sack containing his father's remains, condemning him to bear his father forever, before releasing his two starving dogs. They made short work of the brattish boy, but his soul did not rest quietly. Instead, he returned as a malevolent spirit known as El Silbón.

As a ghost, he still carries the sack across the plains, but he's literally grown even more terrifying since, reaching six meters tall. He hunts lone travelers, particularly drunks or those who cheat on their partners, though not to eat them. El Silbón tears their flesh from their bones, before throwing the bones into the sack. You can tell he's in the area if you hear him whistling, though beware; the closer he is, the fainter his whistle is, while the further away he is, the louder his whistle.

In other legends, he acts as a death herald, turning up at a person's house after sunset. He spends the night counting his father's bones and if no one hears him, he leaves again in the morning and all is well. But if you hear him, you'll be dead by morning. Luckily, dogs can ward off El Silbón, since he hates the sound of their barking. You can also crack a whip to terrify El Silbón into leaving you alone or recite the Lord's Prayer at him. The story is sometimes used to warn violent or cheating men to change their ways, lest they encounter El Silbón. Yet he's also a reminder that family dynamics can be toxic and destructive, leaving behind a violent imprint on the world.

El Silbón Colombia and Venezuela

LA BOLEFUEGO

You marvel at the twinkling light show overhead, as the Milky Way sprays across the immense vault of the night sky. You're not surprised they call this area Big Sky Country. Your companion elbows you in the ribs, his voice insistent in your ear. A ball of fire has appeared a few yards away, dancing from side to side. Curiosity, fascination, and a tiny frisson of fear jostle for your attention, and you move to stand up. If you can get closer, maybe you can get a better look. Your companion forces you onto the ground, holding your head down so you can't see the fireball. "Es la Bolufuego!" he hisses. The need to look at the strange sight wanes now that you can't see it. Time crawls by until your companion finally lets you get up. All that is left of the phenomenon is its image, burned in your memory.

La Bolefuego, or The Firehead, is a legend found in the same Los Llanos region as El Silbón (p.168). In the legend, a ball of fire patrols the plains, looking for unwary travelers—but the reasons for its existence vary.

In one version of the legend, a beautiful woman named Candileja lived on the plains. She received attention from many eligible bachelors, but eventually married a man named Esteban, and had two sons with him: Sigifredo and Esteban Junior. Unfortunately, Esteban Senior was fond of alcohol, and as a musician, often performed at festivals on the plains. On one occasion, he told Candileja that he wouldn't take her with him, though the reason is lost to history. Furious with her husband, Candileja decided that if he wouldn't take her to the festival, then he wouldn't go either. Nor would he go to any other festivals; she killed him with an axe, burying his body on the plains.

> **In the legend, a ball of fire patrols the plains, looking for unwary travelers— but the reasons for its existence vary.**

She devoted herself to raising her sons, ignoring other marriage proposals until Sigifrido reached the age of 14, and Candileja took him as a lover. She kept Sigifrido out of sight, terrified a girl his age might take him from her. When Esteban Junior reached 14, Candileja also tried to make him her lover, but he refused.

La Bolefuego · Colombia and Venezuela

Eventually, time passed, and Candileja died, though what became of the boys is unknown. God punished her for her heinous actions towards her sons by turning her into a fireball who leads travelers astray across the plains. In another version of the story, the fireball is the eternal punishment for a woman who murdered her son after he announced he wanted to become a bishop.

The woman returned from her fiery grave as La Bolefuego, a phantom with flames for hair, who likes to scare travelers by showing them her charred corpse.

A third version of the legend is more sympathetic towards the woman. This story tells of the horrific death of a young woman and her child while her husband was away. Bandits attacked the home and while the woman fought back, they overpowered her. After assaulting her and stealing from the house, the thieves decided to hide the evidence of their crime by setting fire to the house. Cruelly, they locked the woman and her child inside before starting the fire. The woman tried everything to escape, but the smoke overcame her and her child. They died, the woman's pleas to God for help falling on deaf ears. The woman returned from her fiery grave as La Bolefuego, a phantom with flames for hair, who likes to scare travelers by showing them her charred corpse.

Whatever the origin of the fiery spirit, the advice for dealing with La Bolefuego is the same. Do not pray, since prayers attract her attention. Instead, curse the spirit, which counteracts any prayers, or lie face down on the ground.

La Bolefuego 💀 Colombia and Venezuela

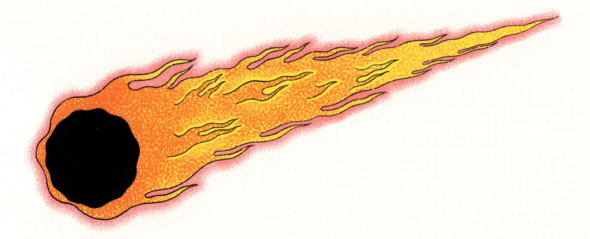

You can also keep your eyes tightly shut, and avoid looking at the fireball until it leaves. It's said to be most encountered in the week before Holy Week, which lies between Palm Sunday and Easter. That said, skeptics have pointed out that the phenomenon's appearance in the summer months could mean it's simply an optical illusion, caused by the interaction of the sun and the dry plains.

> **Perhaps the nature of the spirit is less important than the lesson it teaches, that it can be dangerous to venture into an environment you don't fully know or understand.**

Yet the fireball nature of La Bolefuego, leading travelers from the path across the savannah, has led some to draw comparisons with both the feu follet of Louisiana (p.156) and the will-o'-the-wisp of Europe. These spirits work to lure unwitting travelers into dangerous territory; in Louisiana and Europe, this is the bayou or the marsh, while in Los Llanos, it is the expansive savannah, with its vast spaces and flood plains. Perhaps the nature of the spirit is less important than the lesson it teaches, that it can be dangerous to venture into an environment you don't fully know or understand.

PISHTACO

You've already left the bus by the time you realize you've made a mistake. This is not the street you're looking for, filled with shuttered businesses and shadows between the flickering streetlights. You check your map app and see you've gotten off two stops too early. Still, the alleyway to your left looks like a shortcut to where you want to be. You approach the lane, ignoring the warning screaming in your head, when a figure moves in the darkness. It looks like a fellow tourist, dressed in a football top and jeans. You spotted him earlier, reading a cheap airport novel over lunch at a cafe. Yet now, he doesn't look so innocent, lurking in the shadows at the mouth of the alleyway. A bus trundles along the road and you run back to the stop, fumbling for change as you leap on board. You peer into the alleyway as the bus rolls past, and a pair of eyes glare at you from the darkness. Looks like you just avoided an encounter with a pishtaco.

> **In the colonial era, it looked like a Catholic priest or a soldier, then became a doctor in a lab coat. Now, it adopts the guise of an archaeologist, a businessman, or a tourist.**

Pishtacos are often lumped into the same monster category as vampires, although they differ in some crucial ways. They appear in the Quecha folklore of the Indigenous people of the Andes. The name comes from "pishtay", a Quechan word that means "behead" or "cut into strips". As the Quecha people moved from Peru towards Bolivia, they took the pishtaco legend with them.

The pishtaco always looks the same, taking the form of a tall white man, often with a beard. While its physical appearance has remained the same over the centuries, its clothing has changed to suit the time in which it appears. In the colonial era, it looked like a Catholic priest or a soldier, then became a doctor in a lab coat. Now, it adopts the guise of an archaeologist, a businessman, or a tourist.

Pishtacos behave like white tourists, eating the same food as visitors and avoiding local delicacies. Crucially, they don't speak Quechan, further marking them out as

strangers to the area. Yet at night, they lurk in the quieter, darker, more dangerous places of the world, like alleyways and ruins, and on half-forgotten roads. They attack male passersby before slitting their throats and removing their fat to sell in the cities. In some versions of the legend, the pishtaco puts his victims to sleep using a powder made of human bones. He removes their fat while they sleep, and when they wake up, they sicken and die within days. The only way to defeat a pishtaco is to behead it—which is also a surefire way to dispatch a vampire. Yet the tales of the pishtaco turn it into a cautionary tale, encouraging people to avoid dark, lonely places at night, especially if they're alone.

He removes their fat while they sleep, and when they wake up, they sicken and die within days.

Stories of the pishtaco are incredibly common among the people of the Andes, with many either believing in it wholeheartedly or at least taking the stories seriously enough that they avoid the places a pishtaco is said to frequent. The pishtaco also reflects the region's history, with the change in the pishtaco's appearance reflecting the different white people who invaded the land over time. In 1571, locals accused Spanish priest Cristóbal de Molina of being a pishtaco. They feared he would steal

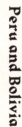

their fat, which would be used to grease church bells or make medicine. According to folklorist Anthony Oliver-Smith, the conquistadors used human fat to treat wounds during the Conquest, so these fears were not entirely unfounded. That the pishtaco originally looked like a priest and now looks like a tourist reveals how the Indigenous population recorded information about these dangerous white newcomers in story form, where it could be easily preserved and transmitted.

The fact that the pishtaco steals fat is also telling, since fat represents life and strength in the Andes. The pishtaco siphons off such strength by stealing the fat of the locals; it's a focused metaphor for colonialism. This explains why this dangerous monster looks like a white man, rather than some of the more fantastical spirits in this book. The ongoing stories of the pishtaco reveal the ongoing generational trauma of colonialism, with the theft of strength and vitality representing the loss of Indigenous sovereignty. It says much that the pishtaco does not appear in sources before the Conquest, although vampiric creatures exist in Peruvian lore.

Perhaps the worst part about the pishtaco, other than the trail of death and violence it leaves, is the fact that he enlists humans to help with the process. The first pishtaco stories were ostensibly spread by locals who were forced to work with pishtacos themselves. While they clearly hated the work, the pishtaco paid them well and they couldn't afford not to do it. Indeed, such stories live on into the 21st century. As recently as 2009, men kidnapped locals in the Huánuco jungle and stole their fat to sell for ritual purposes. Only the capture of three of them revealed the gory practice, and for some in the area, the story proved pishtacos were still in operation. Perhaps they still are.

Pishtaco

Peru and Bolivia

177

EL PEUCHEN

You and your friends reach the edge of the trees and find yourselves in a beautiful clearing. Birds cluster around the pond in the center, bobbing to drink from the cool water. You all find tree stumps to perch on, ready to dig into your packed lunches. Suddenly, the birds dart back into the trees. A vast shadow falls across the clearing, and a strange whistle carries on the still air. One of your friends bolts back toward the trees and the rest of you follow suit, reaching the safety of the forest just as a giant winged serpent swoops over the clearing. The downbeat of its wings sends a waft of blood-scented air into your face and you struggle not to gag until it flies away, further up the mountain. You only re-enter the clearing when the birds do.

El Peuchen is a form of forest spirit—perhaps better described as a monster—that is depicted either as a blue and black snake with red, blue, and yellow wings, or as a snake-shaped bird. It is ultimately a shapeshifter with just one goal—feeding. It feeds on blood, usually feasting on sheep, cattle, or goats, although it will attack humans if they're nearby. Shepherds might blame El Peuchen for dead sheep, while farmers would suspect El Peuchen if their cattle became thin and sickly without any obvious cause. Whatever its target, El Peuchen uses its paralyzing gaze to keep its victim still before it sinks its fangs into its chosen prey.

> **El Peuchen is a form of forest spirit—perhaps better described as a monster—that is depicted either as a blue and black snake with red, blue, and yellow wings, or as a snake-shaped bird.**

El Peuchen is scary in its proportions, bigger than a person, and it is sometimes characterized as being strong enough to knock over trees, raise massive waves, and leave trails of blood through the forest. It whistles as it flies, which at least gives people the chance to find cover before El Peuchen spots them. In some areas, people believe it exudes a substance carried by water or air that causes skin rashes. If it gets into a house, it will kill every resident by draining them of their blood—unless they

El Peuchen | Chile and Argentina

manage to escape. In some folklore, it seems that you can do this only by crossing running water.

But El Peuchen isn't completely invincible. The Machi, the medicine women of the Mapuche people, can defeat the creature using a herbal mixture that stops it from using its paralyzing gaze. In some legends, they perform a secret ceremony to drive El Peuchen away. Another method for getting rid of El Peuchen involves finding its hiding place in a tree, covering the entire tree with a strong cloth with El Peuchen inside, and setting the cloth and tree on fire.

El Peuchen is a fascinating spirit that bridges two different families of monstrous creatures.

The monster appears primarily in the lore of the Mapuche people who are indigenous to south-central Chile and southwestern Argentina, but also Chilote people in the southern half of South America. The earliest written record that is still accessible is in a 1916 Spanish-Mapuche dictionary, compiled by a Spanish missionary named Father Augusta who studied the Mapuche language. It's perhaps worth noting that according to horror writer J. A. Hernandez's translation of the dictionary entry, Father Augusta described El Peuchen as an "imaginary animal". There is an earlier 1765 record that also highlights the presence of El Peuchen in Mapuche legends, though the reference is incredibly brief.

El Peuchen is a fascinating spirit that bridges two different families of monstrous creatures. On one hand, the word "peuchen" also refers to the vampire bat in Chile, which some writers suggest may have given rise to the tales in the first place. Sadly, you can't confuse the two, given the tiny size of the vampire bat and the colossal proportions of El Peuchen! Drinking the blood of livestock is about all they have in common.

El Peuchen Chile and Argentina

180

But on the other hand, its behavior places it in the group of creatures that can seemingly paralyze victims with nothing but a stare. J. A. Hernandez notes similarities between El Peuchen and the basilisk, a North African creature that paralyzes victims with its stare and is sometimes depicted as a bird with a serpent's tail. It also resembles the cockatrice from English folklore, which had a serpent's body and a rooster's head, legs, and wings. Like El Peuchen and the basilisk, the cockatrice could kill with a glare. The link between a paralyzing stare and snakes even suggests the famous Gorgons of Greek mythology, most recognizable in the form of Medusa. The existence of these paralyzing snake-like monsters in different cultures and periods shows how some spirits reappear all over the world.

The link between a paralyzing stare and snakes even suggests the famous Gorgons of Greek mythology, most recognizable in the form of Medusa.

In more recent times, people have linked tales of El Peuchen with El Chupacabra, whose legend only dates to 1995. Its first attack saw eight sheep in Puerto Rico drained of blood. Notably, witnesses described a winged creature that swooped down to attack livestock, although later reports vary. Such monsters explain sudden deaths in both people and livestock, and it's perhaps more comforting to think of them as folkloric pests than real creatures.

El Peuchen · Chile and Argentina

LA MOCUANA

You head along the Pan-American Highway, peering out of the window at the expanse that rolls by. Your friend provides a running commentary as they drive, pointing out features of interest. Suddenly, you spot a woman by the side of the road. The wind whips her long, black hair around her face. You ask your friend to stop, but instead, they accelerate. She isn't trying to hitch a lift or flag down help, your friend explains. The woman is La Mocuana, and she only has revenge on her mind...

The La Mocuana legend dates to the Spanish colonization of the Americas and involves a band of Spanish conquistadors in the 1530s. When they arrived in Sebaco Valley, Nicaragua, they met a friendly Indigenous tribe that greeted them and sent them on their way with plenty of gold. The conquistadors were pleased with the offering and moved on, saving their violence for other parts of the land. Other versions of the story explain that the Spanish crushed any resistance by the people of Sebaco, and the tribe handed over pouches of gold after their defeat. Either way, the story of the encounter and the tribe's wealth reached the people of Spain, and one of the conquistador's sons heard of their generosity. As he wanted to be a priest, he decided to meet this tribe, though no one knows if he had benevolent intentions.

> **The La Mocuana legend dates to the Spanish colonization of the Americas and involves a band of Spanish conquistadors in the 1530s.**

He traveled to the valley, and met the people. As he expected, they greeted him with curiosity and kindness, and he found them as generous as he hoped they would be. Even better, the chief's daughter, La Mocuana, was an exceptional beauty, and it was obvious she'd taken a shine to the would-be priest. Here the stories differ: some versions of the legend stress a romantic element, whereas others suggest the Spaniard only turned his attention to La Mocuana to get his hands on her father's wealth. Another version insists that even if this was his intention, he still fell in love with her. Yet La Mocuana's father would not hear of marriage, insisting the Spaniard was not the right man for his daughter.

The chief was right to distrust him. La Mocuana showed him the location of the tribe's cache of gold to prove she trusted him. Instead of being humbled by this display, the trainee priest tied La Mocuana up and left her in a cave. After blocking up the entrance, he stole the entire cache. Filled with rage, disappointment, and guilt, La Mocuana began to dig her way out of the cave. She managed to do so, but by the time she was free, the Spaniard—and the treasure—was long gone. Betrayed by her lover, and realizing she had betrayed her people, La Mocuana didn't know where to go or what to do for the best. Assuming her people would think she'd been killed, or even that she'd run off with her lover, she wandered into the forest. According to legend, she still haunts the area.

Instead of being humbled by this display, the trainee priest tied La Mocuana up and left her in a cave.

Only La Mocuana is no longer the good, kind, trusting young woman she once was. Now she lurks in the darkness, waiting to lure lone men into the trees with her ethereal beauty. No one knows what she does to these men because they're never seen again. In this way, her story reflects tales of other female spirits that prey on lone men, such as the Sundel Bolong (p.98), Aïcha Kandisha (p.126), and La Ciguapa (p.140). Like La Ciguapa, La Mocuana reflects

La Mocuana

Nicaragua

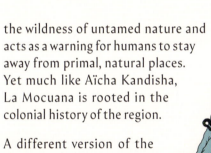

the wildness of untamed nature and acts as a warning for humans to stay away from primal, natural places. Yet much like Aïcha Kandisha, La Mocuana is rooted in the colonial history of the region.

A different version of the legend says La Mocuana haunts the cave, appearing on the nearby road to lure men to their doom inside. Anyone who has encountered her says they can only see her bewitching figure because she hides her face with her hair. Some say they have seen her, dressed in silk, by the Pan-American Highway. Other reports suggest it's impossible to enter her cave because it's also home to a massive bat colony.

La Mocuana

Nicaragua

> **Anyone who has encountered her says they can only see her bewitching figure because she hides her face with her hair.**

Her legend speaks of the betrayal of the Indigenous people by Spanish colonizers, and her ongoing persecution of lone men reflects the revenge she seeks on the man who betrayed her. Many readings of the legend focus on the latter perspective, yet the perils of colonialism are intrinsic to the story. Here, La Mocuana represents collective trauma caused by the conquistadors and whether she was a real person or not, she recalls the violent history of the region every time someone tells her story.

Resources

BOOKS

African & Caribbean Folktales, Myths & Legends – Wendy Shearer
A Natural History of Ghosts: 500 Years of Hunting for Proof – Roger Clarke
The Book of Japanese Folklore: An Encyclopedia of the Spirits, Monsters, and Yokai of Japanese Myth: The Stories of the Mischievous Kappa, Trickster Kitsune, Horrendous Oni, and More – Thersa Matsuura
An Encyclopedia of Fairies: Hobgoblins, Bogies, and Other Supernatural Creatures – Katharine Briggs
Chinese Fairy Tales & Fantasies – Moss Roberts
Ghostland: An American History in Haunted Places – Colin Dickey
Folktales from India – AK Ramanujan
Horror Tales of Japan: 21 Japanese folktales not to be read to children, coupled with (mostly) uplifting cultural commentary – Kyota Ko
Islam, Arabs, and the Intelligent World of the Jinn – Amira El-Zein
Latin American Folktales: Stories from Hispanic and Indian Traditions – John Bierhorst
Never Whistle at Night: An Indigenous Dark Fiction Anthology – edited by Shane Hawk and Theodore C. Van Alst
The Ghost: A Cultural History – Susan Owens
The Runaway Princess and Other Stories – Helen Nde
Song of the Dark Man: Father of Witches, Lord of the Crossroads – Darragh Mason

PODCASTS

Afro Mythos
Afro Tales
After Dark: Myths, Misdeeds & the Paranormal
The Asian Tapestry
By the Fire
Celtic Myths and Legends
The Faerie Folk
The Folklore Podcast
The Folk Tale Project
Ghosts and Folklore of Wales
The Hidden Djinn
Jewitches
Knock Once For Yes
Legendary Africa
Legends From The Pacific
Spirit Box: Folklore, Magick & Spirits
Uncanny Japan
Yes, This Happened

WEBSITES

American Folklore – americanfolklore.net
American Folklore Society – americanfolkloresociety.org
JA Hernandez – www.jahernandez.com/
Folklore Thursday – folklorethursday.com
Mythopedia – mythopedia.com
The Folklore Society – folklore-society.com
World of Tales – worldoftales.com
Yokai.com | The Illustrated Database of Japanese Folklore – yokai.com

186

Glossary

Bogeyman: a monstrous figure, spirit, or being often used to terrify people (usually children) into behaving a particular way.

Brownie: a household spirit found in Scottish folklore that comes out at night and does chores, but can be mischievous or even malevolent if angered.

Curse: a form of wish that something bad will happen to an individual or group.

Demon: an evil nonhuman spirit that appears throughout folklore and mythology. They are often associated with Hell in Christian theology.

Exorcism: the process followed to attempt to eject a spirit from a human body that it has no right to possess or occupy.

Fairy: a supernatural being, common in folklore around the world. Usually invisible to humans, they can be benevolent or malevolent, depending on their own goals. Fairies can grant wishes, but usually require something in exchange.

Folk tale: a story that was originally passed on orally between people. While they often emerge within a culture, many cultures have folk tales with similar story arcs, characters, and motifs.

Jinn: a range of intelligent spirits from the lore of south west Asia and Arabic mythology. They can be both benevolent and malevolent, and are invisible to humans unless they choose to adopt a form humans can see.

Nyctophobia: an extreme fear of the dark.

Phantom hitchhiker: a common legend in which a driver or motorcyclist encounters a hitchhiker who disappears from their car or motorbike, often without warning, before they reach their destination.

Possession: a supernatural process in which malevolent spirits take control of a person's body without their consent.

Reincarnation: in its simplest form, the process through which a soul is reborn into a new body to live a new life.

Shamanism: an ancient spiritual practice in which an experienced practitioner, the shaman, uses trance to connect with spirits in the otherworld.

Shapeshifters: beings with the ability to alter their form. The soucouyant is a shapeshifter because they appear as old women during the day, but transform into a fireball at night. They regain their human shape to pass among humans undetected.

Sleep paralysis: the often terrifying but natural phenomenon in which your mind wakes up but your body is still in the sleep state, and you are unable to move or speak.

Spectre: another word for ghost or apparition.

Spirit: often considered to be supernatural beings, such as fairies or monsters, though some also consider ghosts to be spirits due to their supernatural qualities.

Soul: the spiritual part of a human that is often considered immortal.

Urban legend: a story that is circulated as being true, usually after being experienced by a friend of a friend, or someone equally distant. The story is about an unusual event, and often scary, and they are shared by a wide cross-section of the population. Similar urban legends appear in different countries and contexts, suggesting they share motifs that easily translate to different places. They differ from legends since they are often contemporary in nature, while legends are usually situated in the past.

Vampire: a creature that was usually human and becomes a monster after death, leaving its grave in order to feed on blood and sustain itself.

Witch: in folklore, witches were humans believed to have supernatural powers that gave them control over other people or their environment. They were nearly always viewed as evil.

Index

A

Adams, W. H. Davenport 105
Adze 106–09
Aïcha Kandisha 14, 126–29
Akan people 117
Albania 49
animism 14, 69
Anuman Rajathon, Phya 69
Argentina 179–81
Aswang 64–67
Athenodorus 18–19
Atteberry, Todd 154
Australia 83–85

B

babay 161
Bali 100
banshees 34
Barguest 28–31
basilisks 181
bats 65, 66–67, 117, 119, 139, 180, 185
Belarus 161
Bell Witch 54, 55
Bender, Hans 54–55
Bengali folklore 49
Benin 107–09
blood, drinking 42, 71, 107–09, 117, 129, 133, 179–80, 181
bluecaps 51
Boba 49
Bolivia 175–77
Bonsu, Osei 117
Botchey, Adwoa 109

Brazil 49, 161
Briggs, Katharine 29
Brunvand, Jan Harold 125
Buddhism 69, 91, 92, 93

C

Canada 143–45, 147–49
Caribbean 133, 135–37, 139, 161
cats 21, 30, 46, 49, 72
cautionary tales 14, 22, 25, 41, 88, 93, 100, 117, 125, 173, 176
Central Africa 105
Chaudhury, Rabia 79
Chile 179–81
Chilote people 180
China 71–73, 75
Chukwudera, Michael Chiedoziem 115
churels 141
churiles 133
cockatrice 181
Colombia 169, 171–73
colonialism 14, 66, 100, 121, 127–29, 139, 175–77, 183–85
Commi people 105
corpse candles 46
Côte d'Ivoire 117
counting countermeasures 49, 72, 133, 136–37, 157
Crichton, Michael 139
Croker, Thomas Crofton 34
Crom Dubh 35

D

Daimler, Morgan 34–35
Danquah, J. B. 117
Dickens, Charles 85
Dominican Republic 141
douens 133
Draugr 20–23
Du Chaillu, Paul 105
Dullahan 32–35
Dungarvon Whooper 142–45
Duppy 134–37

E

Egypt 79–81
El Chupacabra 181
El Peuchen 178–81
El Roba Chicos 161
El Silbón 168–69
Emezi, Akwaeke 115
Enfield Poltergeist 55
England 29–31, 51, 55, 181
Eulalia 164–65
Ewe people 107, 108
Eze, Chinelo 115

F

fairies 12, 30, 31, 37, 39, 49, 157
Federici, Frederick 85
Feu Follet 156–57, 173
Fisher's Ghost 82–85
France 27

188

G

Germany 53–55
Ghana 107–09, 117
glaistigs 37
Glámr the woodcutter 22
Greece, ancient 19, 181
Greenbrier Ghost 152–55
Green Lady 36–39
Grettir's Saga 22
Grudge movies 61, 88
Grýla 161
Guyana 133
Gwisin 86–89

H

Harte, Enda 19
Hawai'i 95–97
Headless Nun 146–49
Hearn, Lafcadio 59
Hernandez, J. A. 151, 180, 181
hitchhikers 7, 123–25
Homen do Saco 161
Honduras 161
Horgan, Colin 161
Hupia 138–39

I

Iceland 21–23, 161
Ifrit 78–81
Ilechukwu, Sunday T. C. 115
India 77, 141
Indigenous peoples 14, 84, 97, 120, 135, 175, 177, 180, 183, 185
Indonesia 93, 99–101
Ireland 33–35, 46
Irving, Washington 33
Italy 49

J

Jamaica 135
Japan 59, 61–63, 93
Jiāngshī 70–73
jinn 79, 121, 127, 129, 141
Jumbee 132–33, 135
Jun, Sunhee 87

K

Kaneshiro, Kamuela 96
"knocker" spirits 51
Korea 87–89

L

La Bolefuego 170–73
La Ciguapa 140–41
La Diablesse 141
lagahoo 133
La Mocuana 182–85
La Pascualita 166–67
La Planchada 12, 162–65
Little, Mack 136

M

Madam Koi Koi 110–13
Malaysia 67, 93, 100
manananggals 65
Mapuche people 180
Mary Queen of Scots 38
Matsuura, Thersa 63
Maxwell-Stuart, P. G. 55
Medusa 181
mermaids 136, 141
Mexico 163–65, 167
Mokthi 49
Morocco 127–29
Myling 24–25

N

Naale Baa 76–77
Nde, Helen 109
Nicaragua 183–85
Nickell, Joe 85
Nigeria 107–09, 111–13
night hags 49
Night Marchers 94–97
Norway 22, 25
Nrenzah, Genevieve 117

O

Obambo 104–05
Ogbanje 114–15
Okiku 59
Ole Higue 133
Oliver-Smith, Anthony 177
Olomi, Ali 79
One Thousand and One Nights 80–81
Onryō 12–13, 60–63
Ourkiya, Asmae 129
Owen, Ruth 41

P

Padfoot 30–31
Pantafica 48–49
paralyzing gaze 179, 180, 181
Paris catacombs ghost 26–27
Persia 79–81
Peru 175–77
Phi Hua Khat 68–69
Philippines 65–67
phi spirits 69
Pisadeira 49
Pishtaco 174–77
Poltergeist 12, 41, 52–55

Popobawa 118–21
Portugal 45–46, 161
Preta 13, 90–93
Puerto Rico 181

Q

Quecha folklore 175

R

Radford, Benjamin 121
Ramos, Carolina 45, 46
Ramos, Maximo D. 67
Ridgeway Ghost 150–51
Romania 41–43
Roux, Maria 123–25
Russia 161

S

Santa Compaña 44–46
Sasabonsam 116–17
Satoko, Koyama 59
Scotland 12, 37–39
sea mahmy 136
shamanism 87
shapeshifting 29, 30, 66, 79, 80, 99, 107, 151, 179
Shimizu, Takashi 61
Shubin 50–51
Simmons, Judy 133
Singapore 93
Society for Psychical Research 55
Solomon, King 80
South Africa 55, 123–25
Spain 45–46, 161
Spieth, Jakob 108
Strigoi 40–43
Sugawara no Michizane 63
Sundel Bolong 98–101
Suzuki, Koji 59

T

Taíno culture 139
Thailand 69
Thompson, Camela 41
Thompson, P. A. 69
Togo 107–09, 117
Tokoloshe spirit 55
Tolkien, J. R. R. 23
tommyknockers 51
Tozer, Rev. Henry Fanshawe 42

U

Ukraine 51, 161
Underhill, Doug 148
Uniondale Hitchhiker 122–25
United States of America (USA) 51, 151, 153–55, 157
urban legends 111, 113, 121, 160–61, 167

V

vampires 41–43, 65, 66, 71, 73, 101, 108, 139, 177
Venezuela 169, 171–73
Victoria, Queen 39
video games 22–23, 73, 81

W

Wadstål, Molly 21, 22
Wales 37–39, 46
Walsh, Martin 120, 121
Whelan, Michael 145
whooping boy 136
Wild Hunt 46
Williams, Joseph John 117
will-o'-the-wisps 59, 157, 173
witches 49, 65, 77, 108–09

Y

Yeats, W. B. 34–35
Yuan Gui 74–75
Yūrei 58–59

Z

Zanzibar 119–21
zombies 21, 71, 73

About the author and illustrator

Icy Sedgwick is the host of the *Fabulous Folklore* podcast, investigating the strange and often bizarre world of European folklore (with a focus on the British Isles). She's particularly fascinated by the appearance of folklore in popular culture, but also the ways in which folklore preserves information in an easily transmissible format. In case she tires of all that folklore research, former ghost hunter Icy holds a PhD in Film Studies, after examining the representation of haunted houses in contemporary Hollywood cinema. Like any good folklorist, she has a horseshoe over her door, and she doesn't stray too close to bodies of water...

Mabel Esteban García is an illustrator fascinated by what is hidden under the surface. She studied Fine Art and has a master's degree in ceramics. Years later, she developed her career in illustration. Her first series was named "The Beasts", where she built mythological characters that were half humans, half creepy animals. She has written two comics named "La muda" ("Shed skin") and "Algunas criaturas de agua" ("Some water creatures"). Mabel's work often focuses on the disturbing and macabre of the seemingly normal, the mysterious that everyone keeps within themselves.

DK LONDON

Editor Millie Acers
Designer Isabelle Merry
Managing Editor Pete Jorgenson
Managing Art Editor Jo Connor
Production Editor Marc Staples
Production Controller Louise Daly
Art Director Charlotte Coulais
Publisher Paula Regan
Managing Director Mark Searle

DK would like to thank Florence Ward for copyediting,
Victoria Taylor for proofreading and Joanna Luke for indexing.

First American Edition, 2025
Published in the United States by DK Publishing,
a division of Penguin Random House LLC
1745 Broadway, 20th Floor, New York, NY 10019

Copyright © 2025 Dorling Kindersley Limited
24 25 26 27 28 10 9 8 7 6 5 4 3 2 1
001–345825–Aug/2025

All rights reserved.
Without limiting the rights under the copyright reserved above,
no part of this publication may be reproduced, stored in or introduced
into a retrieval system, or transmitted, in any form, or by any means
(electronic, mechanical, photocopying, recording, or otherwise),
without the prior written permission of the copyright owner.
No part of this publication may be used or reproduced in
any manner for the purpose of training artificial intelligence
technologies or systems. In accordance with Article 4③ of the
DSM Directive 2019/790, DK expressly reserves this work
from the text and data mining exception.

Published in Great Britain by Dorling Kindersley Limited
ISBN 978-0-5939-6690-7

DK books are available at special discounts when
purchased in bulk for sales promotions, premiums,
fund-raising, or educational use.
For details, contact: DK Publishing Special Markets,
1745 Broadway, 20th Floor, New York, NY 10019
SpecialSales@dk.com

Printed and bound in China

www.dk.com

This book was made with Forest
Stewardship Council™ certified
paper—one small step in DK's
commitment to a sustainable future.
Learn more at **www.dk.com/uk/
information/sustainability**